Memoirs of Samuel Hoare by His Daughter Sarah and His Widow Hannah

MEMOIRS OF SAMUEL HOARE

PLATE I

CRAYON PORTRAIT OF SAMUEL HOARE (1751-1825)

From the original painted in 1816 by Josiah Slater, in the possession of
Marlborough Robert Pryor, at Weston, Hertfordshire

Josiah Slater del. 1818

Samuel Hoare
(1751–1825)

Emery Walker Ph. sc.

MEMOIRS OF SAMUEL HOARE BY HIS DAUGHTER SARAH AND HIS WIDOW HANNAH.   ALSO SOME LETTERS FROM LONDON DURING THE GORDON RIOTS

.

EDITED BY
F. R. PRYOR

.

PRINTED BY HEADLEY BROTHERS
BISHOPSGATE LONDON MDCCCCXI

CONTENTS.

2

LIST OF PLATES

PREFACE.

The original MS by Miss Sarah Hoare, from which the first memoir is printed, occupies eighty-nine pages of a small quarto note-book, and was begun in 1825, the writer being then eight and forty There are slight differences in the ink and the handwriting, indicating that there were some intervals of time before it was completed.

This notebook was given by Sarah Hoare to Ellen Toller (daughter of Thos. M. Pryor), who devoted much loving care in their declining years to "the old ladies at the Heath," the writers of the two memoirs. The notes signed E T. are by Mrs Toller

On her death, in 1891, the book passed into the possession of the late Mrs. Richard M Harvey (Adeline Powell), and is now the property of her daughter, Mrs. H. G Buxton, Tittleshall, Swaffham

The notebook also contains copies of letters written from Broad Street during the Gordon Riots of 1780. The originals of these are in the possession of Mrs MacInnes (Anna Maria Hoare), North End House, Hampstead.

A picture painted by Francis Wheatley, and engraved by Jas Heath, is entitled "The Riot in Broad Street on the 7th June, 1780" Tradition has it that a figure in a Quaker-like costume, apparently endeavouring to restrain a rioter, is that of Samuel Hoare

The picture represents a view looking southwards down Old Broad Street, taken from close to where London Wall joins it, and the street opening out of Broad Street on the left hand side, is Wormwood Street. Horwood's Map of London in 1799 shows that the large house at the southern corner of Wormwood Street and Broad Street was numbered 42, and that the numbers 42-33 were the houses between that corner and the Excise Office, which is the high building shown in the distance , so that number 36, where Samuel Hoare and his wife dwelt, is visible in the picture   The numbering of the houses in Broad Street has not been altered since 1799, but Number 36 has been pulled down, and the more northern part of Palmerston House now occupies the site on which it stood

The Memoir by Hannah Hoare is printed from a copy in the possession of Mrs Thomas E Powell   Several copies exist,—the original is not forthcoming.

The family to which the subject of these memoirs belonged appears to have been resident in Ireland since 1649, and to have there joined the Society of Friends during the latter part of the seventeenth century.

It has been stated by Capt Edward Hoare, in his book on the genealogy of the family, published in 1883, that Edward Hoare, great-grandfather of Samuel, who was an officer in Cromwell's army in Ireland in 1649, was descended from the Hore family of Chagford, in Devonshire   This statement, however, was unsupported by any evidence, and has been discredited by recent research. Though some of the evidence which has come to light seems to point to a descent from the Hoares of Northamptonshire, the earlier pedigree of the family has yet to be proved.

Of Samuel Hoare, the elder, whose character and habits are so vividly sketched in the memoir by his grand-daughter, the obituary notice in the "Gentleman's Magazine" for 1796, is as follows:—"Aged 80, at Stoke Newington, where he had lived ever since 1748, possessed of an ample fortune, Mr Samuel Hoare, one of the most respectable inhabitants of that parish, always uniform and consistent in his conduct, strict and steady, but neither bigoted nor troublesome with his strict adherence to the principles of his sect ; of the most irreproachable integrity, always ready to assist and serve the poor, without regarding their religious sentiments, plain, unassuming and unostentatious, always more inclined to withdraw from than to push himself into public notice   A man whom nobody had anything to say against.   His family originated from Cork, and he carried on a large trade with Ireland."

In the "Life of Crabbe," by T. E Kebbel, it is stated (p. 88) " When he came to London he made the house of Mr. Hoare, at Hampstead, his head-

quarters; (p 92) "He continued his annual visits to London down to the
year 1825, staying usually with the Hoares at Hampstead   .   Among
others with whom he used frequently to meet were Wilberforce, Joanna Baillie,
Miss Edgeworth, Mrs. Siddons, Wordsworth, Southey, Rogers, Lord Holland, etc ,
and every season he accompanied the Hoares to some seaside place—the Isle
of Wight, Hastings and Ilfracombe being their favourite resorts "

A drawing, dated November, 1822, represents Crabbe walking with Sarah
Hoare in the field by Cliff House, Cromer   With them are Mrs. Opie, Samuel
Hoare, Wilberforce and Dr. Lushington   On the wall are two children, said
to be those of Sophia (Grizell) Powell.   A copy of this picture is owned by
W. Douro Hoare, and reproductions of it have been made.

Among the silhouettes here reproduced are those of Mrs Galton and Mrs
Schimmelpenninck, about whom, as they are not mentioned in the Memoir, a
word of explanation may be required ·—Lucy, daughter of Robert Barclay, of
Ury, M.P., and of Lucy (his wife and cousin, daughter of David Barclay, of
London), married Samuel Galton, of Duddeston House, Warwickshire, in 1777 ;
she died in 1817.   She and her daughter, Mary Ann Galton, who married Lambert
Schimmelpenninck, and left interesting memoirs, were intimate friends of
Samuel Hoare.   Her grandson, Francis Galton, whose death took place in
1911, had a world-wide reputation as a man of science.

Mrs. Fry (Elizabeth Gurney), speaking of Mrs Schimmelpenninck, says —
" She was one of the most interesting and bewitching people I ever saw, and I
never remember any person attracting me so strongly " (" Gurneys of Earlham,"
Vol. I , p. 86)

Sarah Hoare was a painstaking pupil of William Hunt, whose studio was in
Hampstead Road, London   Several of her water-colours—fruit and flower-
pieces, and drawings of children—copies and originals in the style of her
master,—are extant.   Two of her portrait-groups are reproduced in this
volume (pages 34 and 50)

The " Portrait Gallery," p. 34, was painted by Sarah Hoare, as a collection
of likenesses of her father's friends and visitors.   The portraits are copied

Preface

from well-known originals   There being no likeness of Samuel, her grand-father, it seems that the wit of Sarah supplied the omission by a drawing of "The Witch of Endor calling up the ghost of Samuel"   The fireplace was drawn from one at the "Heath," the rest of the room being imaginary

In Sarah Hoare's common-place book, now belonging to Miss Wilhel-mina L Powell, are poems by Mrs Barbauld, Mrs Opie, J Wordsworth, and others   In it Crabbe addresses Miss Hoare, on "Vaccination," in seventy-two lines of verse.

Miss W L Powell also possesses a very charming little relic of Sarah Hoare's mother, in the shape of a green shagreen case, containing an inkpot and silver penholder, the latter being made in six pieces to enable it to go into the case, which measures only two inches by one-and-three-eighths inches.   On the top of the case are the initials, S G in dots of silver.

An album of silhouettes collected by Hannah Hoare, and inscribed "Hannah Hoare's Profile-book," was left by Mrs Toller to Miss Janette M. Powell, Hawsted, Buckhurst Hill, by whose kind permission nine of them are here reproduced.

The only members of the family, which has been connected with Hampstead since 1790, now resident in that suburb, are Mrs MacInnes and her sister, Miss Hoare

Mrs MacInnes remembers that one of Sarah Hoare's great interests was her girls' school, in what is now called East Heath Road   This was probably at the time the only school for poor girls in Hampstead   The children sat in the gallery of Well Walk Chapel, dressed in a sort of uniform   The site of this Chapel is now occupied by Christ Church.

The Heath, now called Heath House, has passed into the hands of Lord Iveagh , and the Hill, occupied by Francis Hoare, up to the year 1895, is no longer owned by Sir Samuel Hoare, Bart , and has been entirely rebuilt. Mrs. Toller lived at what is now called Foley House, East Heath , on the opposite side of the road a block of flats called "the Pryors" stands on the site of a house and garden formerly owned by Thos Marlborough Pryor, and occupied by his second son, Robert, until the year 1863.

For many of the notes I am indebted to Mr Joseph J. Green, formerly of Stansted, Essex, and now of Goldwyn Lodge, Clive Vale, Hastings, the author, with Mr. Charles Wilmer Foster, of a " History of the Wilmer Family," which contains much information as to the families of Hoare, Bradshaw, Harman, Woods and others mentioned in these Memoirs

I have to thank Mr Edgar Powell for his work in seeing the book through the press, and for the compilation of the pedigree

To Mr Emery Walker, of the Mall, Hammersmith, I tender my best thanks for his skill in the production of the plates.

F. R PRYOR

WOODFIELD, HATFIELD, HERTS,
    May, 1911.

PEDIGREE.

Samuel Hoare=Grizell, dau. of Jonathan Gurnell,
b. 1716, d. 30 Aug. 1796. | of Ealing, d. 7 Dec., 1802.
Merchant of London and
of Paradise Row,
Stoke Newington.

—1 Sarah=Thomas Bradshaw   1 Joseph,   3 Jonathan=Sarah Beswick   **Samu**
d. 1813 ⋏   d. 1810   (1750-1774)   (1752-1819)   b.1751, m. 1776
—2 Margaret=Joseph Woods   d. 14 July, 1825
d. 1821   ⋏   d. 1812   of Hampstead
                             Sarah   Partner in
·3 Grizell=Wilson Birkbeck d. 1812=Will. Allen, d. 1843   d. unmarried.   Barnett, Hill,
d. 1835   Barnett & Hoar
—4 Mary, unmarried   **Subject of**
d. 1817.   **Memoirs.**

Sarah   **Hannah**= Thomas Marlborough Pryor,   **Samu**
b. 29 July, 1777,   b. 18 Aug., 1779,   of Hampstead, b. 1777,   b. 16 Jan., 1783,
d. 21 Oct., 1856,   m. 25 Nov., 1802,   d. Mar., 1821,   of Hampstead,
at Hampstead.   d. 30 Ap., 1850,   son of John Pryor,   m. at Tasborough
Writer of the   of Baldock.   Meeting,
1st Memoir.   24 Dec., 1806.
                                       d, 24 Dec., 1847.

————Marlborough=Eleanor Rogers.
(1807-1869).
————Robert=Eliz. C. Wyrley-Birch.
(1812-1889).⋏
————Henry Hoare.
(1814-1841).
————Ellen=Charles Toller.
(1810-1891).
————Caroline=David Powell, son of David Powell,
(1816-1865). ⋏   of Loughton, by his first
                           wife, Mary Townsend.

PEDIGREE.

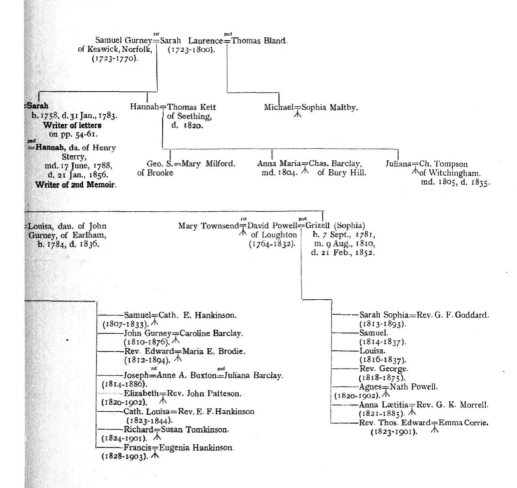

Samuel Gurney=Sarah Laurence=Thomas Bland.
of Keswick, Norfolk, (1723-1800).
(1723-1770).

=Sarah
b. 1758, d. 31 Jan., 1783.
Writer of letters
on pp. 54-61.
=**Hannah**, da. of Henry
Sterry,
md. 17 June, 1788,
d. 21 Jan., 1856.
Writer of 2nd Memoir.

Hannah=Thomas Kett
of Seething,
d. 1820.

Michael=Sophia Maltby.

Geo. S.=Mary Milford.
of Brooke

Anna Maria=Chas. Barclay,
md. 1804. of Bury Hill.

Juliana=Ch. Tompson
of Witchingham.
md. 1805, d. 1835.

=Louisa, dau. of John
Gurney, of Earlham,
b. 1784, d. 1836.

Mary Townsend=David Powell=Grizell (Sophia)
of Loughton   b. 7 Sept., 1781,
(1764-1832).   m. 9 Aug, 1810,
d. 21 Feb., 1852.

Samuel=Cath. E. Hankinson.
(1807-1833).
John Gurney=Caroline Barclay.
(1810-1876).
Rev. Edward=Maria E. Brodie.
(1812-1894).
Joseph=Anne A. Buxton=Juliana Barclay.
(1814-1886).
Elizabeth=Rev. John Patteson.
(1820-1902).
Cath. Louisa=Rev. E. F. Hankinson
(1823-1844).
Richard=Susan Tomkinson.
(1824-1901).
Francis=Eugenia Hankinson.
(1828-1903).

Sarah Sophia=Rev. G. F. Goddard.
(1813-1893).
Samuel.
(1814-1837).
Louisa.
(1816-1837).
Rev. George.
(1818-1875).
Agnes=Nath Powell.
(1820-1902).
Anna Lætitia=Rev. G. K. Morrell.
(1821-1885).
Rev. Thos. Edward=Emma Corrie.
(1823-1901).

PLATE II.

PORTRAIT OF SARAH HOARE (1777-1856).

From the original water-colour drawing by George Richmond, painted in 1840, in the possession of Mrs. Thos. E. Powell, Uppercross, Reading.

Sarah Hoare
(1840)

From the original by...

A MEMOIR OF SAMUEL HOARE.
BY SARAH HOARE, HIS DAUGHTER.

My beloved father breathed his last the 14th of July, 1825, and this day, the 1st of August, I am able with a tranquil mind to commence this memoir.

To me he was dearer than any human being, and if those who read what I now write, having remarked the strength of my affections, and the irritability of my natural feelings, are surprised by my present calmness, let them be assured that it arises from no effort of my own, but from the goodness of God, who has promised peace to those who love Him I have endured sleepless nights and suffering days, when I only dreaded the possibility of losing him, so unutterably dear to me. I went through agonies when I saw him oppressed by disease, I have been ill for months from excessive anxiety, but in all this anguish I was enabled to seek to the Almighty for help ; to cast at least some portion of my care upon Him who careth for me

I had consolation in believing that He knows from experience our infirmities, and that He is not hasty to punish even an excess of affection so peculiarly sanctioned by the Divine command I now find rest ; my nights and days, though tinged more or less with affliction, are no longer miserable I earnestly desire to make the best use of the heavy dispensation, and have no fear for the future, persuaded that I shall once more be happy in this world, or in the next, and conscious of the mercies and good providence which have attended me all the days of my life.

My father was born the 9th of August, 1751, in the first house in Paradise Row, Stoke Newington,[1] in the end next the village His father, Samuel Hoare, was a merchant in the city, distinguished for his good sense and great integrity. A striking fact illustrates this, for the house in which he was a partner having (it was feared) undergone an heavy loss in consequence of the great earthquake at Lisbon, he was surprised to find the principal merchants on the Exchange coming forward to meet him with offers of assistance to any amount

To this business he was introduced by the connections of my grandmother, whose name was Gurnell I know little of his early life He was born in Cork, and engaged young in the Irish provision trade. His uncle was a dean,[2] and I have heard him say that he was one of five brothers, each having a religion different from the others Their mother was a Quaker which probably determined his own religious opinions.

His paternal grandfather was a Major in Oliver Cromwell's army, and distinguished himself so much that the Protector gave him as much land in Ireland as he could ride round from sunrise to sunset I have this anecdote of our common ancestor from Sir Joseph Hoare. I confess it has little the air of truth The estate[3] certainly did not descend to our branch of the family.

My grandfather and grandmother married young, and had a large family of children On his marriage his dress was not smart enough to please his wife,

[1] In 1903 I found Paradise Row, Stoke Newington, with many houses as they must have been for 130 years without much alteration Here and there bow-windows have been put in, and stucco put on The New River runs opposite, and on the other side is Clissold Park, the house in it being that built by Jonathan Hoare A stone from the lodge has the date 1790 on it I called on "the oldest inhabitant," Mr William Beck, a Friend, of whom I had heard from Mr Fox, of Headley Brothers, Printers He had attended lectures given by William Allen in his house, now a school It is probably the house that Samuel Hoare (died 1796) lived in In W Allen's life it is stated that after his marriage with Grizell Birkbeck he lived in a house once occupied by Samuel Hoare.—[EDITOR]

[2] Miss Hoare was mistaken as to the "dean"—Edward Hoare, elder brother to Joseph Hoare, of Dunkittle had several children, of which the third was named Deane Hoare, after Sir Matthew Deane—[Cf "Families of Hore & Hoare," p 10]

[3] Among the grants of land under the Acts of Settlement and Explanation (1666-1684) there is one, enrolled 18th October, 1667, to Captain Edward and Lieut Abraham Hoare, of the ruinous walls of a castle and part of the lands at Tougher and elsewhere, amounting in all to 3,468 acres (Report of Committee respecting Public Records of Ireland, 1821-1825, p 133).

.

Plate III.

SKETCH BY LANCELOT SPEED

Of the house in Paradise Row in 1911, residence of Samuel Hoare, Senior

⟩

SAMUEL HOARE'S HOUSE, PARADISE ROW.

and he told her that he would change it in any way she pleased at that time, but would alter it no more,—and he scrupulously kept his word   He looked, ever since I can recollect him, like the pictures in the reign of George II ,— a large white wig, with rows of curls, a mulberry-coloured suit, the coat with wide sleeves opening very high from the wrists with sugar-loaf buttons, black worsted stockings and a shirt without a frill, so curiously plaited, that only the old servant Mrs Molly, who lived in the family from youth to age, was considered equal to the task of putting this last finish to her master's costume.   She also knew how to minister to many of his other peculiarities,—to weigh out his chocolate with scrupulous care, and the sugar required for every basin-full, and these little parcels were carefully packed for journeys   A small table was placed for him to eat his breakfast, whilst the rest of the family took their meal at the large table   His habits were singular, and he rarely thought the occasion great enough to interrupt them importunately.

After breakfast he regularly smoked his pipe, and I am told, never bestowed any caresses upon his children till they were old enough to bring him one.

At nine he went to town in a green coach, with red wheels, and without regular springs, and he kindly sent to his neighbours with offers to convey them

He was at home again before two, and generally told us of the health of our friends in London.

At two we dined, unless the hour was changed to three for the accommodation of company   Two boiled turnips on a pewter plate were set before him, and one was eaten before he partook of fish or meat ; and a pint of porter stood by his side.

At certain hours he took exercise in the garden, and if the weather would not permit, did curious dancing steps in the dining-room

Every summer he used to visit Scarborough, making a week's journey, with post-leaders to his own horses   The conveyance was insupportably tedious to his family who accompanied him.

But with all these oddities he had sterling good sense from which all his descendants profit, I doubt not, in some degree.

To many of the peculiarities of the Society of Friends to which he belonged he never conformed, though he left off card-playing as his family became old enough to be influenced by his example.

His religious views were liberal ; he said he would never believe anything of God inconsistent with His attributes of wisdom, justice and mercy. He was strictly moral in his conduct, rarely ruffled in his temper, able to advise others to their advantage, and remarkably correct in all money transactions without meanness

He was able to give respectable fortunes to his children, allowing his sons one-third more than his daughters.

In his manners he was very grave, and when he relaxed a little and played with his grand-children, few of us were at ease enough to be merry.   He expected attention and obedience   Such was my reverence for him that I can scarcely believe it possible that anyone could have approached him without awe, but his character was not calculated to excite affection.

My grandmother was a mild, excellent woman. We loved her tenderly, for she was always considering what would make others happy.   I see her now in her Duffield[1] cloke and black bonnet, trudging after the poor she assisted, and making visits to her neighbours in the Row who required attention.

She had the humility not only of a Christian, but that kind of indifference to appearances which was often embarrassing to others. She busied herself in little household concerns for her amusement, and I remember a laughable story of her reminding Mrs Goddard,[2] who had risen in the world, of some former occupation, in the midst of a large company, blind to the blushes she occasioned, and without the slightest consciousness of having given pain   This lady's brother, Mr. Henry Hope[3] (who acquired an immense fortune),

[1] A coarse woollen cloth which came from Duffel, a town near Antwerp

[2] The wife of John Goddard, Esq , who died at Woodford Hall, Essex, 26th May, 1798

[3] Mr Henry Hope, of Amsterdam   He was apprenticed in 1754 to Gurnell Hoare & Co , remained with the firm till 1760, and died in 1811, leaving a fortune of more than a million sterling

was once a clerk in my grandfather's counting-house, and spoke of this without hesitation.

Attention to little delicacies formed no part of my grandmother's character ; but those who knew its excellences could easily dispense with them She was not a mental companion to her husband, but was all he wanted in a wife. As a mother she was kind to all her children, but a little partial to those who most needed her help. My aunt Woods, who married a man of small fortune, and had bad health, was her great favourite.

My grandmother had a sister,[1] a widow, my aunt Harman, a striking contrast to herself, hard to please, exacting attention from all , and, if not the terror of those who approached her, inspired them with great awe From what I remember of her, she was a comely and dignified old lady, deeply imbued with self-import-ance, and talking nothings with the voice of an oracle

Joseph, the eldest son in my grandfather's family, lived to the age of five-and-twenty. He was always spoken of with affectionate regret Showing symp-toms of consumption, he was ordered to Lisbon for his health, and died on his passage home. He was buried at Falmouth, to the great satisfaction of his mother, who could not bear the idea of a watery grave ; and the great kindness exhibited by the Fox's on this melancholy occasion was the commencement of that friendly intercourse with has since subsisted between the two families

My grandfather had two other sons who lived to grow up, and four daughters My father, who was the second son, was sent with his elder brother to school at Penketh[2] in Lancashire, when only five years old, and they came home but once in the year for the holidays I know not the date when they were taken from this school, and my father was placed with his younger brother Jonathan at a Seminary in the Grange Road[3] kept by John Riveaux, who afterwards removed with his pupils to Kennington.

[1] Hannah, daughter of Jonathan and Grizell Gurnell, and widow of Jeremiah Harman, of St Martin's Lane, London and Boston House, Ealing, she died 17th April, 1795

[2] Penketh lies between Warrington and Widnes on the Irwell For an interesting account of Gilbert Thompson's school, when S Hoare was there, see the Memoirs of John Coakley Lettsom, M D , by Th J Pettigrew —[Vol I , p 7]

[3] At Highbury

I know few school anecdotes   One day to escape punishment after having told a lie, my father climbed a tree to conceal himself, and stayed there a considerable time, meditating on the great fault he had committed, and then, convicted by his own conscience, came down from the tree, and submitted to the flogging.

Another story was the punishment of greediness by disgrace.   The apple pies were not sufficiently large to furnish two helpings to the whole school, so the boys who ate fastest sent their plates first to be replenished.   He pocketed the first helping (as he trusted) unobserved, and boldly sent his plate for a second, when the master with a loud voice put him to open shame, calling out, " Sam, eat that which thou hast got in thy pocket first "

I remember that in after life he thought he could still relish schoolboy dainties, and stopped at a frequented shop for a tart once delicious to him But it proved, alas ! the object of disgust rather than delight

He was always fond of birds and humane to animals ; and having (as he thought) killed a cat who had killed his pigeons, was made so unhappy by finding the poor animal still alive and able to crawl, that he never forgot the suffering it occasioned him.

He was taken from school between fourteen and fifteen, and bound apprentice to Henry Gurney,[1] a Norwich woollen manufacturer   Of this period of his life he often spoke with much pleasure.   He became acquainted with the Gurneys, and in love with Nancy Rogers, who is still living, and for whom he always maintained a regard   She was several years older than himself, and they never intended to marry

I have heard him describe his smart blue coat, put on for the first time, and the accompaniment of a powdered bob-wig, and the destruction of this finery by falling into the water and being covered with duck-weed.   The loss of a new coat could have been no trifle with his moderate finances   I question if his father allowed him more than £20 per annum , and after having received a lively

---

[1] Henry Gurney, son of John Gurney, of Norwich and founder of the Bank of Gurney & Co, Norwich—[Cf Gurneys of Earlham, I , 18)

remonstrance intreating further supplies, my grandfather wrote to Henry Gurney enquiring if the extravagant demands of his son were the result of dissipation and bad company. The reply must have been satisfactory, for his early religious impressions were such that he was strictly moral in all his habits.

He went occasionally on excursions of pleasure with the Gurneys, and they who had more money at command paid his expenses

At this period his friendship commenced with Wm. Bleakley, an excellent man, and a minister among Friends,—and with John Ransom.

How far my father was educated as a Friend I do not know, but as his feelings were susceptible, and he was thrown amongst excellent people of this persuasion, he was much influenced by them, constantly went to meeting, and, though incapable of imbibing their narrow prejudices, highly valued their many virtues

He spoke with great pleasure of my grandfather, Samuel Gurney[1] a paralytic, but whose mind was so exalted his society was delightful to him.

He first read " Paradise Lost," in a summer-house in a garden in Norwich belonging to John Freshfield, with feelings of the highest enthusiasm , and it is remarkable that in after life this sublime poem was by no means a favourite, though not thrown aside, like the school tarts, with dislike

He was at this time peculiarly awake to religious feeling, and as he gave to his Creator the best thing that he had, listened to the only claim made by His Heavenly Father, " My son, give me thine heart," he was preserved from the strong temptations to which feelings so animated must have exposed him had they missed their right direction. When principle was firmly established, the same vivacity no longer existed.

In the works of grace, as well as of nature, how frequently do we experience the sufficiency without the superfluity.

The religious character which he maintained through life was unalterably fixed at this time.

I know not the exact date of a long journey he took into the North of

[1] Son of Joseph Gurney, of Keswick, by Hannah Middleton, his wife, He died 1770.

England with Mr. J. Gurney[1] They travelled in the accoutrements of Friends, and their hats served as passports from one Friends' house to another ; so that travelling on horse-back, and scarcely stopping at an inn, their expenses were a mere trifle

In 1772 my father's apprenticeship was expiring, and my grandfather wrote to him to enquire his views with respect to the future He was accidentally turning over a directory and observed that there were only two partners in the house of Bland and Barnett, 62, Lombard Street, and told his father the result of this remark, and that he should like to be a banker. Proper application was made, and it was determined that he should be received a third partner in the business. I know not what fortune he received from my grandfather, but his connections were so good that the business was considerably extended by this new partnership, and my father devoted much of his time and mind to his occupation.

Lombard Street must be a good school for the study of character, and in this instance was also discipline for the temper, for Mr Bland[2] had a very passionate disposition, swore tremendously, and exacted almost servile obedience from those whom he could command, compelled his youngest partner to be exceedingly punctual with respect to hours, and permitted so little time for recreation that his health materially suffered from close confinement.

His habit, was, however, to spend his evenings at my grandfather's, and when he was detained later than usual in town, to lodge at the house of a man mamed Freeman, whose wife was niece to Dr. Fothergill Here he became acquainted with Alice Chorley,[3] six years older than himself, sister to Mrs Freeman, and as the Freemans had it in their power to secure a permanent lodger in Mr. Dillwyn,[4] and my father much preferred Mrs. Chorley, he changed his abode, and went to live with her and her husband, when unable to get into the country

---

[1] John Gurney of Norwich

[2] John Bland, b 1723, d 1788 *Cf Gentleman's Magazine* for 1788, II , p 939

[3] The wife of John Chorley, of Tottenham She was an elder among the Quakers, and died 1828, aged eighty-two

[4] Possibly the Quaker Philanthropist, William Dillwyn

Mrs. Freeman was by no means reconciled to this change, and was so jealous of the preference shown to her sister, that almost a dispute took place,—indeed it was some time before they were completely reconciled.

I can describe Mrs Chorley a comparatively young woman, for she is mingled with my earliest recollections ; lively, sensible and healthy in her appearance, and with too good a countenance to be plain, notwithstanding her high cheekbones and prominent mouth. But I can only guess what she was as a young woman when this acquaintance commenced   Much less can I define the friendship which subsisted between two persons whose minds seemed formed for each other.

She loved her husband, and made him her companion, though he had a peculiarly weak, dull manner   He used to ride me about in a chair, and was happy in his own insignificance, and took great delight in the attentions paid to his wife

My father always wrote to her under cover to him, but he was too delicate to peruse what was addressed to her. She had an insatiable love of reading, and had great power over the tastes and habits of a young man in whom she found such marked superiority of intellect, and so many engaging qualities.

They constantly read together in the evenings, and, when absent from each other, the books they were separately engaged in furnished new food for their conversation when they met, as they made extracts for each other

So clever a woman as Mrs. Chorley naturally would draw to her house many young professional men, and the class of society in which she moved, and her taste for the information which at that time could not easily be gained from women, occasioned an openness and freedom of discussion which we should not think very refined, and which my father's nice sense of female propriety would have made him dislike in a wife, though habit made it not disagreeable to him in a friend whom he so highly valued.

When she was ill he used to nurse her, and he found her so capable of understanding him when he was nervous, that he often preferred remaining with her to going to his family at Newington.

Every thing and every person were freely talked over between persons so congenial. They had no secrets from each other, and I am persuaded that, for a time, neither party had a thought that this indulgence of mutual affection could be dangerous.

At last he began to suspect that the results might not be strictly right, and this suspicion hastened his marriage. On this point she was also consulted, and was surprised to find he was attached to the long-necked girl who became my mother.

His friendship for Mrs. Chorley, if it had not religion for its basis, was the union of two persons who strongly felt its operating power ; and in conversation as well as letters there were many comments on Friends' sermons, and, I doubt not, many expressions of heartfelt piety.

The conversations [are] now forgotten, or remembered only by her, the letters long since burnt with tears from both parties as memorials of a friendship too intimate to fall into the hands of anyone but themselves.

To the young she was particularly pleasing, not only for her great love of a garden (in which she and her husband used to work like Adam and Eve, and liberally bestow their fruits and flowers upon us), but from the amusement furnished by a mind so original

She told stories of second sight and supernatural appearances with such firm faith that mine (my faith) is influenced by it to this day. But what may be thought credulity was not the result of fear, for she had great personal courage, thinking it was a mercy that she was preserved from killing a man with the poker, who was holding a pistol at her husband's head, with the intention of robbing the house at Lavender Hill, where they resided for some years. And, talking to another of these six housebreakers of the future judgment awaiting crimes like his, she agitated him so much that he told her he would hear no more ; whilst the drops of sweat dropped down his face. He gave her back her watch, and would not suffer her trinkets to be touched, but he persisted in the robbery, and she never heard of him again.

My father also had a curious adventure with thieves, which strongly marks his habitual attention to truth

He was on the road between London and Newington in a stage-coach one night, and having some suspicion that it might be attacked by highwaymen, concealed his watch. The coach was stopped and a pistol presented. The passengers gave up what they had about them, and he gave his money, and being asked for his watch felt for it in his fob, and said, " I have none." But, before the men went away, recollected where the watch was hidden, but not his motive for concealing it ; and said, without reflection, " Yes, I have a watch ! " and gave it up to the thief, advising him at the same time not to expose himself to detection by taking it He hesitated for a moment, and then went off with it

This story was made in conversation ridiculous enough, and attributed to scruple in having told a lie to a highwayman. No desire of preserving the watch would have prompted him to say what was false, but folly only would, on such an occasion, have recanted what was thus spoken inadvertently.

I know not whether he was most distinguished by love of truth, or freedom from scruple.

At about the age of twenty-four he began to think seriously of marrying. Jane Hustler,[1] from the North of England, had been the object of his boyish attachment ; but she told him she could place no confidence in love at nineteen.

The impression made upon him by the eldest daughter of his friend, Samuel Gurney, of Norwich, was of a more permanent nature He saw her contributing to the comfort of a paralytic father, who died when she was about thirteen.

A few years after, her mother, whose maiden name was Laurence, married again to Thomas Bland, who had been in the counting-house of her former husband.

They went an excursion into Devonshire, where my father joined · them ; and notwithstanding the alarming account my mother received of the temper of her intended husband from Mrs. Bland (the wife of his partner in business), she suffered herself to be convinced of its utter falseness, and the marriage took place at Norwich Meeting the 15th of May, 1776.

[1] Cf. p 18

I have been looking at the marriage certificate.[1]   Of the persons who witnessed the ceremony, how few are now in existence !   Of how little importance
are the short contracts, and fleeting occurrences of life !   How can they concern
us, so that our names may but be written in heaven !

I could scarcely make out the few relations that remained alive   Who could
Sarah Hoare be ?   My aunt Bradshaw long since dead ; Hannah Gurney, now
changed to Kett, and a widow ; my aunt Birkbeck I so long knew as Grizell
Hoare, that she appeared to me less strange than anyone

Mrs Chorley had assisted my father in furnishing his house, No. 36, Old
Broad Street.   She told me she took delight in going about with him to choose
furniture, and that she had taken the greatest pains to fill a little garden at the
back with roses.   I am sure they never could have flourished in a climate so un-
genial

She keenly felt my father's marriage as a privation to herself, but gave him
up with generosity, and attached herself to my mother, with whom she had
constant intercourse. .

My mother was not pretty, but her person was pleasing.   Just the middle
height, with a round hand and arm.   Her hair lightish, nose thick, and an in-
different complexion ; but dark hazel eyes which I have been told were exceedingly beautiful.

I remember her very gentle voice and manner, indicative of great sweetness
of temper, and Mrs Chorley says she had good sense   She was very nervous
and had delicate health [so] that she required and received consideration.   She
was educated by an excellent and religious mother ; and had much domestic
affection and tenderness in her nature almost by inheritance [so] that I doubt not
my father, who had been brought up in a much rougher family, gained many
amiable feelings from this happy connection.

Living in the heart of London, old friendships were kept up, and new ones
formed   My mother had some fortune, and their circumstances in life, though
at first narrow, were constantly improving.

[1] This was signed by ninety relatives and friends besides the contracting parties

We had two maidservants and a footman, besides a nurse, and I never recollect a time when disagreeable attention to economy was thought necessary.

Let the young who read this memoir believe what my father found by long experience of life to be true, that persons used to money best know how to use it. Men who marry poor gentlewomen, and women who connect themselves with needy husbands, must never expect to save a fortune, but will probably find what they possess endangered, or hastily run through   Some degree of equality in point of fortune is highly desirable

My father took the liveliest interest in American politics, and was so zealous for her independence, that he shed tears on first receiving the news of General Burgoyne's[1] army laying down their arms, the 13th of October, 1777

He always spoke of the distinguished men engaged in this contest with the familiarity of old acquaintances, and of the places where the battles occurred as though he had been present.   This made the proceedings of the House of Commons highly important to him, and might have been the origin of the amusement he always derived from politics, and his more than common acuteness with respect to political economy, and its connection with finance,—his own particular concern.

Yet he was by no means partial to the Americans as a people.   Their transactions in trade displeased him   If they have escaped some of the glaring vices of the mother-country, they have not the high sense of honour and integrity which distinguish her higher orders   Inhabiting a portion of the earth where everything in nature is on a mighty scale, the mind bears no resemblance to the soil, but is contracted by narrow prejudices, and obscured by selfish habits, destitute alike of the spirit of adventure and the refinements of a long-established government.

My father and mother were neither of them strict Friends, but sufficiently so to make a point of attending Meeting both on Sunday and week days   And as my grandmother Bland was a minister, I doubt not some sacrifices were made

---

[1] John Burgoyne (1722-1792), General and Dramatist, surrendered to Gates at Saratoga 17th October, 1777

in compliance with her wishes.   I know this to have been the case after our birth.

I was born July 29th, 1777   My sister Hannah, August 18th, 1779.   Grizell, September 7th, 1781.[1]

I doubt not my mother was disappointed that we were all girls, for I well remember her telling me in a sorrowful voice before her last confinement, that she thought she should have one more girl and then no more children.

My brother was born January 14th, 1783.   My father was so delighted with this event, that he hastened to his friend Mrs. Chorley that she might share his pleasure

" I have too much good news," he said, " for one day   The birth of a son, and peace concluded with America "

How soon was gladness changed into deepest grief !   How soon was this faithful friend who witnessed his delight, sent for to sooth his heart-rending agony whilst he sat speechless mourning the death of my mother !

Nothing could be less calculated upon than this event, for ten days after she was put to bed no unfavourable symptom appeared.   Dr. Orme attended her, who had been with her in all her confinements ; and my grandmother Bland was in town, nursing her.

I saw her the morning of her death, and remember saying to her that she did not look as usual   She had not her pretty night-cap, but was considered recovering.

My father was at Meeting, and her mother at Clapham on a morning visit to her first husband's niece, Mrs. Barclay.

My mother was getting up, and one of her attendants was fastening her shoe, when she said, " I am faint ! " and fell back in the easy chair.   My father was sent for immediately, and also Mrs. Barnett, who was used to be with her in illness ; and a medical man, a Dr. Inns, was called in as being the nearest at hand   Some spirits were put into her mouth, but I doubt if she could swallow.

---

[1] Grizell Hoare, afterwards wife of David Powell, dropped the name of Grizell and adopted that of Sophia by which she always signed herself.   Cf p 29

PLATE IV.

PORTRAIT OF SARAH HOARE (1777-1856)

From a drawing at Weston

.

Sarah Hoare

When my father came to her he found her utterly insensible, and she soon expired without a struggle.

It is scarcely possible to imagine a greater shock to the feelings of a young man so ardent in his affections to be hurried in one quarter of an hour from a state of the highest earthly enjoyment (at a moment when I am persuaded that he was lifting up his heart with gratitude to the Giver of all good) to a depth of wretchedness which only those who have experienced it can conceive

I was five years-and-a-half old. Our nurse gave us our dinner in the nursery as usual, telling us with tears that our mamma was not well. After a time we were sent for. I sat by my father on the blue drawing-room sofa I now remember turning my face to the end which had brass nails My uncle Jonathan was sitting opposite. I know not if anyone else were in the room

I cried a little when my father told me I had lost my mamma, and he then said, " Take away the children, I cannot bear them "

My grandmother persuaded him to go into the room and take a last look of her whom he had loved so tenderly ; but the impression was so painful that I believe, unless it was accidental, or at a distance, he never again looked upon a dead body

My mother died in her 27th year, in Old Broad Street, where she had resided with my father from the time of her marriage, excepting for two summers which were spent at Welling's Farm at Newington.

We now spent part of our time at my grandfather's, and the rest in town, till the house there was given up, and a small one taken in Paradise Row, that we might be under the care of my aunts,' and though they did not live with us they tried to make my father's new home as pleasant to him as they could

I was too young to understand my father's affliction, or to know what was meant by death. I asked Mrs Molly if the dead came to life again. " Yes," she said, " in the time of miracles "

I knew not what miracles meant, but I prayed that my mother might come to life again. My theological opinions had certainly not been taken much pains

' Grizell afterwards Mrs Birkbeck and Mrs Hoare —[E T]

with by either parent. But I thought I gained from nurse that there were three states after death, and hoped my mother, if she were not in heaven, might at least be in that middle state which was free from suffering.

How little can those who instruct children understand the impressions they make   My mother wished to instil early piety,—I remember sitting on her knee whilst she told me the story of the fall.   And I listened with so much interest, that she was encouraged, and read to me the beginning of Genesis   But I could not understand the language, and the charm was broken

She taught me to read the Testament, but she did not teach me to pray   But either God or nature dictated the first prayer I ever made, " to be preserved from fire ! "

I perfectly recollect waking in the night with the curtains apparently in flames, not at first comprehending that this effect was produced by a fire in Leadenhall Street.

It was from my beloved father that I first became acquainted with the great truths of religion, the Supreme God and Saviour, the happiness of the righteous, and punishment of the wicked.   And I remember having been much impressed by my own misconduct,—but the impression was short.

Though the mixed government under which we lived was unfavourable to the dispositions of children, supreme love and veneration were established in our hearts for my father before we could comprehend their meaning.

He used to spend much time with us, and when he had been detained late in town, would come into our nursery and talk to us when we were in bed, sometimes accompanied by his friends Mr. Taylor and Mr W. Gray[1].

A great point was made in our education that we should speak truth and love each other , but my father was unfavourable to much early instruction.

He taught me to write himself, but he had a distaste or disapprobation of much accomplishment.   I remember Mrs. John Gurney[2] combating the point with him.

---

[1] Walker Gray, of Southgate   Married, 1787, Frances H Harman, daughter of Jeremiah Harman
[2] Elizabeth Gurney, a first cousin —[Cf. " Gurneys of Earlham," I , 163]

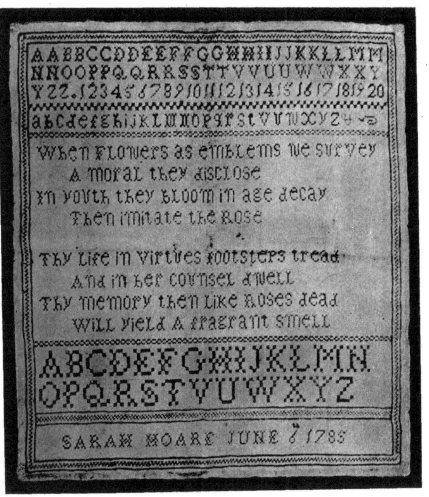

SAMPLER WORKED BY SARAH HOARE.

It was not, however to the interests of domestic life that he was exclusively devoted at this time. Earlier than almost anyone in this country he espoused the cause of the distressed Africans, and, in making his will, bequeathed a legacy to any Society that might be founded with the view of redressing their wrongs

A committee was formed May 22nd, 1787, and be became one of its few members[1].

The immediate abolition of slavery was considered by thinking people a destructive measure, even if it could be carried, and the sole object aimed at in the present was to abolish the slave-trade

Zealous and indefatigable were the first promoters of this important cause Letters were written, visits were made by a small party of obscure men to those who had power and influence. I think the first publication was a sermon by Porteus, Bishop of London[2], which he permitted them to print, awakening the attention of the public, and interesting it in the cause of humanity

Horrible engravings of the interior of a slave-ship were pinned against the walls of our dining-room, and time and money and feeling were liberally expended by these first promoters of an undertaking which has since engaged the attention of every nation in Europe, and [is] being crowned with sufficient success to give sanguine expectations that the results may surpass all human calculation.

My father told me, after this committee was formed, that if he could but see two points carried—the abolition of the slave-trade, and the general establishment of Sunday schools—he should die contented

In this last excellent charity he was engaged with the late Mrs Trimmer[3], and with her encountered the opposition of the ignorant and bigoted

[1] The little band of labourers who first formed themselves into a Committee to promote the great work of abolition, were William Dillwyn, George Harrison, Samuel Hoare, Thomas Knowles, M D , John Lloyd, and Joseph Woods Their first meeting was held in 1783 The mode they pursued was enlightening the public mind, and some of their efforts proved highly useful In 1787 a Society was formed upon a more extended scale, when the names of Granville Sharpe, Thomas Clarkson, and several others were added to the committee —[" Life of Wm Allen," 3 vols , 1846, I , p 20]

[2] Beilby Porteus, Bishop of London 1787-1809

[3] Mrs Sarah Trimmer (1741-1810) daughter of John Joshua Kirby. She was a well known authoress, and wife of James Trimmer, who resided at Brentford

He also assisted in a plan for sending the Blacks[1], who infested the streets, to form a settlement in Sierra Leone, but I fear this benevolent intention occasioned the destruction of many of them

His interest in politics and public affairs was increased by the new connections to which these humane objects naturally led   And as all great undertakings in this country can only succeed by a combination of numbers, the mixed society he was drawn into greatly enlarged his mind, gradually weaning it from family prejudices, and the habits of a sect

I do not remember exactly the time when he exchanged his house for the second in Paradise Row, next to that in which he was born, and not quite so near that which my grandfather had for many years occupied, with large iron gates. Here, however, much of our time was passed, and we were constantly associated with the children of my aunt Woods, and with those of my aunt Bradshaw[2] when they were in England.

I went four times to Scarborough with my grandfather's family. In the summer of 1877, I think, my father came to us there, and made with us a delightful excursion to Knaresborough to see the dripping well, with which he was much pleased, and also with a visit he made to Undercliff, where John Hustler resided with his wife and two daughters.

---

[1] From W Allen's Life, edition 1851, page 93

1814   The African Institution, though it conferred many advantages on the Black settlers, did not answer all the wishes of its founders, in consequence, as stated in its first report, of "its fixed determination not to engage in commercial speculations"   The settlers found great difficulty in parting with their produce to their satisfaction, and they had no way of conveying it to England so as to make the most of it themselves

On this point Mr Allen differed in opinion from some whom he regarded with love and reverence, and to carry out his convictions, a new society was formed, as the following notice imports

First month, 24th —A meeting at Plough Court of an important nature for Africa   Thomas Clarkson, George Harrison, Samuel Hoare, jun , T F Forster, B Forster and Charles Barclay, met, and we formed "A Society for the purpose of Encouraging the Black Settlers at Sierra Leone, and the Natives of Africa, in the cultivation of their Soil, by the sale of their produce "

1815   Fifth month, 4th   Committee on African concerns at eleven, at W Allen's house   Samuel Hoare, Sen , was in the chair , his son was also present, together with Robert Barclay (brewer), G and A R Barclay, the Forsters (bankers), T F Buxton, etc.

[2] Thomas Bradshaw, who married Sarah Hoare, was a Linen Manufacturer of Mile Cross, Newtownards, Co Down, Ireland

The youngest, Sarah[1], was a sensible and superior woman, and I think my father considered a little if she might not suit him as a wife , but if he did, the decision was in the negative.

I now approach the period of my father's second marriage The youth of my present mother, for she was scarcely nineteen, made the connection apparently an imprudent one to those unacquainted with the parties ; but he had sufficient insight into her character to discover the germ of excellences which under his care and culture would ripen into good fruit.

She was the daughter of Henry and Mary Sterry, who resided at Bush Hill [near Enfield] in the summer, and Hatton Garden in the winter.

As we had not the usual prejudices with which children are imbued against second marriages, when my father told us his intentions, I heard them with pleasure, and rejoiced that I too should have a mother like other girls with whom I was associated.

The marriage took place June 17th, 1788, and my mother was established as mistress in our house at Newington.

Our beloved nurse was parted with on this occasion, as my aunts thought the measure necessary, and a governess set over us , and my father had to listen to many a complaint, and pacify many a quarrel, in consequence of this new government.

For my mother we felt affection from the first, for she was attached to my father with sufficient enthusiasm to love all that was dear to him ; but to the necessity of submitting to wholesome restraint, after having been instructed by an indulgent aunt, and the still harder necessity of exerting our faculties and learning long lessons, we bent with a very ill grace

My father was equally firm and mild, and time and patience effected what could only have been accomplished immediately by an harshness which would have lessened affection.

We passed a month this year at Brighton.

[1] Sarah b 1765, daughter of John Hustler, of Bolton House, near Bradford, a merchant in the Wool Trade

Mr. Bland, my father's partner in business, died this year ; and James Barnett, nephew to Mr. Barnett, was taken in his stead.   Mr. Hill, who had been a clerk in the house, had for some time been in the business as a partner, and was at first a great relief by sharing the labours of Lombard Street.

My brother had a dangerous illness during our residence at Newington, and my mother nursed him through it with the greatest care and tenderness.

In the autumn of 1789 we first went to Cromer ; my father had been there before with his friend, Mr J. Gurney, and the place furnished such poor accommodation that one of their beds was obliged to be lengthened with chairs before it could be slept in

Our house in the churchyard did not abound in comforts ; and we particularly needed them, from having caught the measles from one of our menservants.

My father had happily had the ill before, and nursed my mother and all of us with the greatest care and tenderness   He went about from room to room feeding us with peaches on a fork.   Oh, how like to what we did for him in his last moments ; my eyes fill with tears when I think of it.

He was delighted with Cromer.   A zealous sportsman, he found abundance of amusement.   And, though from having no land, there was some jealousy between him and those who had, the pleasure far out-balanced the pain.

This Norfolk excursion united us still more closely to our own mother's relations, and so much attachment subsisted between them and my present mother, that many were the advantages derived from this intercourse.

My grandmother treated her with the greatest confidence and affection, and my aunt Kett[1] became her intimate friend.   From her husband, my uncle, we all gained much ; he had so much acuteness of observation and love of literature, that the pursuits and tastes of our family owed much to him and his children

Visits to Norfolk were long enjoyed by us all, and our time was divided between Norwich, and Seething, and Cromer, in the neighbourhood of which the Barclays then resided

[1] Hannah Kett, née Gurney, wife of Thomas Kett, of Seething, Norfolk

We also made short visits to Earlham.

My father's earliest friendships were thus kept up, and entailed upon his children to the happiness of all parties.

He had not been long returned from Norfolk, when my father was seized by a nervous affection which greatly alarmed my mother. Dr. Sims, his old friend, attended him, and Dr. Reynolds was called in

I know not at what period to date the commencement of this great drawback to his happiness. He compared it to St. Paul's thorn in the flesh, sent to buffet him. It infringed upon every comfort, slackened every exertion, made society fatiguing, and solitude irksome ; often converted wholesome food into poison, and the most nauseous drugs into the greatest dainties Like St. Paul too, he used to say, " I die daily," for it continually presented the images of death, and produced its most distressing fears. But here it stopped. It had no power over his understanding—always strong enough to resist the phantoms of imagination, though not to conquer them. It could never force him into follies to obtain relief or forgetfulness ; and never soured a temper ever under control

Unless suffering under the heavy pressure of this direful complaint, he always appeared cheerful, and continually said it was sent to humble him, and that he should be too happy without it.

The physicians sent him to Bath in December, 1789, and he was taken so faint and ill the first stage, that at Brentford he was obliged to get out of the carriage at an apothecary's, and lie on the floor till he got better.

We all went the journey with him—slept at Salt Hill, and were three days getting to Bath An excellent house was taken for us—No 14 in the Crescent—and the water was happily productive of the benefit expected from it

To suit his invalid habits, we dined at this time at three o'clock, and he used to walk every day after dinner up and down the Crescent.

In these walks he used to encounter an handsome middle-aged man, with hair tied and powdered and curled at the sides, a cocked hat and gold-headed cane. He had been much on the continent and in the West Indies, and knew more of life from experience than my father, who enjoyed the information he gained from him.   Thus commenced the friendship between our family and Mr. Milford, afterwards productive of so much interest.

The medical man who attended my father thought the New River, running so near our house at Newington, might be injurious to his health ; and that an higher situation would be preferable.   And in June 1790 we removed to our present house at Hampstead, quitting Newington entirely.

The change was important to the whole family.   In separating from my grandfather and aunts, we were taken from under very powerful influence, from the constant society of Quakers, from long-established domestic habits— continued because no one had the courage to break them—and we were thrown upon new acquaintances, some of whom became friends ; and we had new desires, both parents and children—to become more like our neighbours.

In quitting Newington, we took leave of a relation I have not before noticed —Mrs Harford,[1] niece to my grandmother.   Her kindness was so great to us when we were motherless that her house was continually open to us, and a frequent scene of amusement and pleasure.

The first years of our residence at Hampstead were marked by few events. My father sent my brother to school at Bradenham in Bucks,[2] under the tuition of Mr. Lloyd, a clergyman of the establishment—a step very dissatisfactory to Friends who then predicted what has since taken place, that he would quit their Society.   But the narrow education then given by sectarian schools happily did not meet my father's views or wishes.

We took a delightful journey into the North of England in June, 1793 ; delightful, at least, to those who were free from pain and anxiety.   To my mother it was far different, for my father was seriously ill at Doncaster, and thought of returning home from thence.

Nervousness pursued him wherever he went, and threatened to baffle every project, though in this instance it did not succeed, for he was well enough to proceed to Scarborough.

[1] Beatrice, wife of John Harford (1736-1801), daughter of Jeremiah Harman, by Hannah, his wife, daughter of Jonathan Grizell Gurnell.
[2] A village on the Chiltern Hills a few miles from High Wycombe

Henry Meyer sc.

Anna Laetitia Barbauld

Emery Walker Ltd sc.

My uncle Kett's family joined us there, and we took Hackfall and Studley and Matlock on our way home, which we reached the 13th of August

In 1794 we became acquainted with Mrs Barbauld,[1] who has been for the remainder of her long life a source of interest and pleasure to us all Her high intellectual attainments and willingness to convey information, were advantageous to those of all ages with whom she conversed My father's prudence, however, made a stand with respect to myself, not approving of too much intimacy with a woman whose religious and political opinions might warp a young person (who had little judgment) too strongly.

This year we were also introduced to her friend, Dr Priestly,[2] previous to his settling in America. My father often spoke of his oily softness of manner covering his natural asperity. I can only remember his spare form and brown bob-wig

We went again to Bath in the spring of 1795, and to Tunbridge Wells in the autumn, which my father thought useful to his health.

He permitted us in the winter to go to the play for the first time. Decidedly objecting to theatrical amusements,—not as evil in themselves, but drawing the young into scenes of temptation, and encouraging vice—he saw no wisdom in disquieting his children by deciding for them, without permitting them to exercise their own judgment.

In this, as in most other cases, he appears to me to have exactly pursued the right path. Certainly the results have been what he most approved.

He scarcely ever was in a theatre himself, and never accompanied us.

In the spring of the following year, 1796, we were introduced at Mrs Barbauld's to Amelia Alderson[3]. whom my father had only known as a girl ; also to her friend Dr. Batty. Her lively manners and amusing talents, I suspect, a little blinded my father and mother to the influence she had on the younger

---

[1] Anna Lætitia Barbauld (1743-1825), poetess and miscellaneous writer, only daughter and eldest child of John Aikin, M D , wife of Rev Rochemont Barbauld

[2] Joseph Priestly, LL.D (1733-1804), the eminent Theologian and Physicist

[3] Amelia Alderson (1769-1851), novelist and poetess, daughter of James Alderson, M D , married John Opie the painter in 1798

branches of the family. I doubt not, however, we were gainers from her many good qualities, if we lost something by what was of a more questionable nature.

Mrs. Knowles,[1] who was also a very amusing companion, came to stay with us; and we had a visit from Wm Savory,[2] from America with whose sermons we were more pleased than with the preaching of any minister amongst Friends whom I remember. The simplicity and genuine excellence of his character made him a delightful companion.

My grandfather's health had been declining for many months, and my father's visits to him were frequent, for no son could be more dutiful, and his attentions were received with cordiality and approbation For five months they were painful and affecting, for my grandfather's superior mind gradually declined. At last his recollection was nearly gone, though I believe he knew the persons about him.

On Tuesday, September[3] 30th, 1796, an express arrived in the evening with tidings of his death. This was not received with great pain by anyone. My father always considered that the mind was the man, and never desired prolonged existence, either for himself or for others, when this was lost.

Melancholy visits were paid to Newington by us all, and we attended the funeral on the Tuesday following, at Winchmore Hill, the village where my mother had been buried

It was affecting to see children and grandchildren following our common parent to the grave Some heirs of his understanding, and others established in the world by his wealth and prudence. But feelings of tenderness he did not excite, for they did not belong to his character.

---

[1] Mrs Mary Knowles (1733-1807), a Quaker, a brilliant conversationalist, intimate with Dr Johnson —["Dict Nat Biog"]

[2] William Savory a celebrated Quaker minister of Philadelphia died 1804 His journal was published in 1844 It was through his instrumentality that Elizabeth Fry became converted and a Quaker in principle and practice —[Cf "Gurneys of Earlham," I , 89]

[3] Capt Edward Hoare gives this date as "30th of 8th month," which would be August and not September ("Families of Hore & Hoare," p. 37)

There was one among us who could have shed no heartfelt tear, but whose improvidence made even the death of such a father an unspeakable relief   I mean my uncle Jonathan,[1] whose affairs were extremely perplexed

Though engaged in the excellent business which was once my grandfather's, he spent far beyond his income, and was engaged in transactions which a parent with so high a sense of honour would have regarded with the highest disapprobation.

His circumstances were made known to his family not long after this period, and proved the greatest vexation my father ever knew   They called forth his forbearance and generosity.   Many thousands were given by him to pay my uncle's debts, who unmindful of all this assistance, continually deceived him, and made promises which he broke when it suited his own convenience.

My father frequently alluded to the answer of our Saviour when the question was asked him, " How often shall my brother trespass against me, and I forgive him ? " and persevered in fulfilling the Divine command from time to time, till it looked as though the seventy times seven would be literally fulfilled

Though my uncle was conscious of the uneasiness he gave, and lived in a state of half-intoxication, friendly intercourse was not entirely stopped between the two families.   No quarrel ever took place between the brothers, and on the death of my uncle's only daughter, he and my aunt spent a week with us at Hampstead

How strange that the sons of one man, so nearly of an age, cast so much in the same mould, should differ so essentially from each other !   In person, height and manner, they bore sufficient resemblance to be mistaken, and my uncle's florid complexion might, at the first glance, be more admired than my father's finer features, and much finer form   But the ethereal spark, given by

[1] Jonathan Hoare, merchant of Throgmorton Street, partner in Gurnell, Hoare & Co   He built Clissold Park house, which after his financial collapse came into the hands of the Crawshay family (iron masters)   A Miss Crawshay married Rev Augustus Clissold, a Swedenborgian, and inherited the property   She died without issue, and Mr Joseph Beck urged the desirability of the purchase of the Park by the London County Council, who eventually bought it   At one time all the inhabitants of the " Row " were Friends   Vincent house was built by Joseph Jackson Lister   Mr Beck mentioned the names of Smith, Capper (still there) and Bevan —[EDITOR]

8

the Creator to shine more and more till the perfect day, beamed in the countenance of the elder brother, whilst in the younger it was obscured by intemper-
ance and self-will—its powers confined to low objects, and its hopes apparently
bounded by a narrow world

We went to Norwich and Cromer the autumn of this year   My father took
care to prevent our being too intimately associated with our relations, the
Gurneys of Earlham, who enjoyed much more liberty than he approved for us,
and spoke upon subjects connected with religion in a manner he so greatly
disapproved, that he desired they might be excluded from our conversation.
His prudence had the wished-for success, for, though he could not prevent our
being fascinated by so new a world, nothing that we saw in them interfered with
our filial obedience, or materially shook the religious sentiments in which we were
bringing up.

On Sunday the 26th February, 1797, Mr. Barnett came to us in the morning
and brought us the astonishing tidings to a banker, that the Bank of England
had stopped payment   No unreasonable fears or anxieties disturbed my father
on this new occasion, but he became more than ever interested by the financial
system of this country, and, I believe, wrote and published in the newspapers
some excellent remarks on the subject   He had conversations with persons in
power who esteemed his opinion, and spoke occasionally in the Bank Courts with
great good sense and self-possession.

His manner of speaking was good, and worthy of the matter which was
listened to with the attention it deserved.

In the autumn of this year his discernment and judgment were the means
of breaking a marriage engagement which had taken place between my uncle
Michael Bland,[1] and a farmer's daughter, who became insane   Sacred as promises are, it was my father's decided opinion that they ought not to be fulfilled
(when the wishes of either party were in favour of their being broken) until an
explanation was made by the party desiring to be free   False delicacy on a
point so important as a marriage-engagement for life ought not to be permitted

[1] Michael Bland, only son of Thomas Bland —[See Pedigree]

Christopher Wordsworth.
(about 1820)

William Wordsworth
1820

to embitter happiness, and risk the destruction of every better feeling and principle. It is far better to encounter the unmerited censure of the world than the
reproaches of conscience, in affecting to desire and enjoy the constant society of
one from whom we should thankfully be separated.

In the autumn of 1798, the daughter of one of my father's oldest friends,[1]
Mr. Charles Lloyd, came to our house for the first time   I mention the circumstance because she peculiarly called forth my father's sympathy in after life,
not merely from the superiority of her understanding, but from her great
suffering from nervous complaints similar to his own.

His tormentor had suspended its violent attacks for nearly four years, but,
in consequence of a return, we set out in the beginning of 1799 for Bath, which
we had not visited for four years   Though my father left home a great invalid,
he returned almost well.

At Bath our intimacy was renewed with the Milfords   We also became
acquainted with Mr Warner,[2] and Col. Barry,[3] and Hannah More.[4]   We spent
one evening with her and her sisters   My father had much conversation with her
on religious subjects, and, though they disagreed on some points, he had so high
a respect for her that he would not suffer us to repeat what we had heard to her
disadvantage.

To the young neither herself nor her sisters were engaging companions   Five
old maids living together in Pulteney Street—four of them dragged into notice
by the talents of their younger sister, and at this time destitute of the polish
of good society, and indulging eccentricities without restraint—were but too
open to the attacks of ridicule.

One sister, Mrs. Sarah, was a politician ; Mrs. Betty, housekeeper to the
family; the wig of one was departing from the head, had not a sister, more alert
than its wearer, kindly replaced it

---

[1] Priscilla, wife of Christopher Wordsworth, D D , brother of the poet, Master of Trinity College,
Cambridge

[2] The Rev Rich Warner of Bath (1763-1857)

[3] Colonel Henry Barry (1750-1822), engaged in the American war, celebrated for his despatches, was
at the battle of Bunker's Hill   Left the army in 1794 and retired to Bath —[" Dict Nat Biog "]

[4] Hannah More (1745-1833), religious writer and philanthropist

Mrs Hannah More's superiority was conspicuous.   The tone of her voice
was soft and pleasing ;   her manners were more refined, though tinctured with a
party slang offensive to good taste ;   and her conversation bespoke the superiority
of her understanding   She was not pretty, but her eyes were dark and lively,
and her countenance varying with expression.

In the autumn of this year we were in Norfolk, and saw my Grandmother
Bland for the last time.   In the winter (of 1800) my father was anxious about her
from an attack of cold   On the 13th of December he brought us the following
account from my uncle Kett.

" Norwich,

"December.

" Dear Brother,

" I am this moment returned from Botolph Street, where I have been with
all my children.   At the request of my mother Bland, we were introduced.   She
told us she was perfectly easy both in body and mind, and wished to see us to
take her leave.   She then adverted in grateful terms to the kindness she has
received from my father, as her guardian.   She then came to her present situation and made many remarks and expressed her earnest wishes for our good, and
desired for us the blessing ' of the everlasting hills ' , said that she was satisfied
she was now entering into a place of rest, and concluded in the words of Addison,
desiring us to see how a Christian could die."

"Nothing can be more desirable than this state of mind, but the stretch of
exertion it requires in those who have a value for her, and are around her, makes
me very anxious for my wife."

" I think, from the ease with which my mother expressed herself—I mean
comparatively so—the strength of her voice, and the steadiness of her pulse, she
is not so near a close as she herself apprehends ; though should the dropsy
invade her lungs she may go off suddenly."

" I have written thus far from the circumstances of the moment, but shall
keep my letter open to give you the latest account "

" Half-past four. I am now returned from seeing my wife   After my mother had seen the servants of the house, she had some quiet sleep   When she awoke, she became extremely sick, but this went off soon, and she appears in much the same state as for some days   But she takes so little, she must weaken very soon   Still I am inclined to the opinion that she may survive two or three days."

On the Monday following (two days after) we received the sad tidings that my grandmother was no more

Affecting as this was to us all, a trial still nearer home prevented us from feeling it as we should have done at another time   My sister Grizell,[1] (now called Sophy), had caught an influenza cold, accompanied with an erysipelatous sore throat, from S Bradshaw, who had been staying with us ; and the ill produced a violent affliction of the head, which came on like an ague, at a particular hour in the day.   When it left her, it was succeeded by a long hysteric.

The day on which we received the last account from Norwich, she was in a state nearly of insensibility for five hours, and I, who had staid by her the whole time, was so much agitated by her recovery, that I ran downstairs to my father, and affected him to tears—much to my regret, for he ever felt but too keenly the sufferings of those he loved, from which it was the duty, and ought to have been the practice, of us all to shield him as much as possible.

My sister slowly recovered her health.

This year is memorable in history from the peace with France   My brother, who had been for some time learning business in Lombard Street, hastened one morning to Hampstead with the good tidings

When Mr. Fox, whom my father never cordially liked, now came into power, he did not rejoice with the Whigs.   To him he was not the delightful companion so deluding to others   He had once dined at our house with some of the gentlemen belonging to the Slave Committee, but said nothing worth remembering   Talents, however, could have never compensated in the upright mind of his host

[1] See note ante p 14.

for the deficiency of that moral integrity which they ought to have embellished instead of opposed

In the summer of 1801 we made a delightful tour to the Lakes of Cumberland and Westmoreland with my cousin, George Kett, and in the autumn my father's eldest sister, Grizell, married Wilson Birkbeck

In the succeeding year, November 25th, 1802, an event much more interesting to my father took place—the marriage of my elder sister Hannah, to Thos Marlborough Pryor

All parties were pleased with this alliance, and his being of the Society of Friends was particularly agreeable to my father's feelings, holding, as he did, that the religion in which we have been educated should never be changed but from some important reason ; and considering that no morality is so pure as that which is practised by Quakers as a society.

Conceiving it utterly impossible for the human mind to be divested of prejudice, he considered his own favour of those in which he had been educated as a thing of course ; and he thought that persons who relinquished their early habits often desired to return to them in after life, when another change might be highly detrimental to their families.

The marriage took place at Tottenham meeting, and we did not need a sermon (of advice to her who was about to leave the paternal mansion) from Thos Shillitoe,[1] to impress us with painful feelings on this first separation.

My father loved us with so much tenderness that the wedding day was anything but joyous. He exerted himself to procure for his daughter and son-in-law a house[2] at Hampstead, that he might have the pleasure of constant intercourse.

The character of my new brother was calculated to call forth the affection of all with whom he was connected The warmth and simplicity of his heart, and cheerfulness of his temper combined with the pleasure he took in field-sports,

---

[1] A celebrated Quaker minister and philanthropist (1754-1836) —[See "Life of William Allen," I , 167]

[2] Belsize, now called Hillfield (E T) Still standing near the Vestry Hall They afterwards lived at Lower Heath House

PLATE IX

PORTRAIT OF HANNAH HOARE (MRS THOS M PRYOR)

From a painting at Weston

Hannah Hoare
(Mrs T. M. Pryor)

Emery Walker Ph. Sc.

Thomas Marlborough Pryor

and manly exercises, made him an agreeable companion to my father, and a welcome inmate in his house, as well as a kind relation.

A family cloud—though not of the heaviest nature—soon succeeded this sunshine   At two in the morning of the 7th of December [1802] my Father lost his mother.   I had seen her the day before, and she appeared as well as usual Sudden death had always been her desire ; she dreaded living to be burdensome to others.   She was sick after I left her, but went to bed comfortably, and took some broth at eleven   Between one and two she told the servant who slept in her room that she was faint, and hartshorn was given to her ; but her appearance was so changed that my aunt Mary was fetched directly, and got into the room in time to see her mother expire—but without being able to ascertain the moment, so great was her quietness.

She had for many months experienced symptoms of decline   Her breath was so much affected that medical men suspected an ossification of the heart, and she had one or two violent nose-bleedings   Still she had not been sufficiently an invalid to keep the house for many days together

My father was very low, but bore his loss with composure   He loved his mother tenderly, and was more overpowered returning from her funeral than I almost ever saw him   She was buried at Winchmore Hill, by her husband's side, on the 15th, in the eightieth year of her age

At Christmas, 1803, my brother was taken into Lombard Street, as a partner ; the insanity of Mr. Barnett, the head partner in the banking house, was a source of great difficulty and disquiet.   Tranquil in his manners, and free from hereditary disease, this calamity could have been little anticipated   My father rode over to Wanstead to the assistance of the family, and learnt that they had been alarmed by his having given orders to cut down trees in Wanstead Park.

Mrs. Barnett was so anxious that her husband should remain in business, notwithstanding this direful indisposition, which rendered him no longer a responsible being, that my father found it no easy task to convince her of the necessity of dissolving the partnership   A separation, however, did take place within the year, and (the partnership) could never be recommenced,

though Mr Barnett recovered his faculties a considerable time before his
death.

His eldest son, George, was taken into the firm, and agreeing perfectly well
with my brother, his old school-fellow, they excited great jealousy in Mr. Hill,
who required more indulgence for his son, than they were disposed to give
him

This son had recently (1806) been taken into the house, and fixed a time for
his holiday which my brother had previously determined to spend in Scotland
with a party of pleasure [1]   So great were the discontents of all parties, that my
father was compelled to think and act with decision, and after much trouble
compelled Mr. Hill and his son to retire Christmas 1806

My brother's great unwillingness to give up this excursion, was his attachment to my sister (in-law) then Louisa Gurney   I know of no event which gave
my father more pleasure than the engagement of his son to the daughter of his
old friend

With perfect confidence in her principles, and a persuasion that she would
make my brother happy, he was pleased with her being, like my mother, a Norfolk
woman, and interested himself much in procuring for them an house at Hampstead that they might be established near him

It was particularly important to him to have those whom he loved within
reach, for travelling, and even long drives, excited so much indisposition, that
no trifling object tempted him to encounter them

The last long journey we made was into Devonshire in 1804 ; he bore a few
days at the Isle of Wight tolerably well, but when we proceeded to Totnes, he
became so seriously ill with cholera morbus, that we were much alarmed and I
went to the apothecary in the middle of the night

Home and rest, however, restored him to a moderate degree of health.   He
would not hear of a private marriage for my brother, which was at first proposed,
but wished himself to be present ; we accordingly made a journey into Norfolk

[1] Fowell Buxton, John Gurney and Louisa Gurney were of the party   Hannah Gurney writes July
16th, 1806, " We set off in three chariots with Sam and Louisa in a whisky behind us "—[Gurneys of
Earlham, I , 150, 157]

PLATE XI.

SILHOUETTE OF LOUISA HOARE, NÉE GURNEY.

From Hannah Hoare's Profile-book.

10

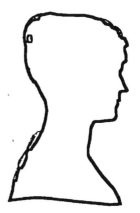

Louisa Hoare
1818

in mid-winter, and witnessed the ceremony at Tasborough¹ meeting on Christmas Eve, 1806   Hannah Evans preached upon the text " Give me a blessing.   Thou hast given me a south land, give me also springs of water."

The south land has indeed been their portion, and has been so refreshed with springs of living water, that they have not only enjoyed the Divine blessing, but have been enabled to extend refreshment and help to others in no common measure.   Time has fulfilled the promises of hope, and earthly happiness, though not sought after as the chief good, has been the result of endeavours reaching to much nobler ends

The large dining-room at Earlham was dressed like a church with holly and Christmas for the entertainment of guests who feasted on swan ; and the following day my father and mother returned to Hampstead.

Our house had been considerably enlarged the preceding summer, and added to the pleasure and convenience of us all ; indeed the marriages in the family made this addition necessary.

My father's first grandchild, the eldest son of my sister Pryor (Marlborough), was born the following March, 1807, and the first of December the same year the eldest son of my brother, (Samuel) ²

Our habits from this period became more fixed   We dined out but little excepting with our relations, and seldom varied our hour of four   We went regularly into Norfolk in the autumn, and to Bath in the winter.   To this place my father was not only indebted for some relief from indisposition, but he became acquainted with many persons whose society gave him pleasure

Here he met Dr. Currie³ of Liverpool, and Dr Maclaine,⁴ one of the most fascinating old men I ever knew   His animal spirits rose above the infirmities

¹ Pronounced " Taysboro "
² See Pedigree
³ James Currie (1756-1805) a Virginian trader until the American war   Physician at Liverpool from 1780, advocated the abolition of slave trade
⁴ Archibald Maclaine (1722-1804), a divine, co-pastor to the English church at the Hague (1747-96) Note from "The Early Married Life of Maria Josepha, Lady Stanley" (Ed Adeane, Longmans, 1899) Letter from Sarah Martha Holroyd (" Serena ") to M J S , Bath, November 13th, 1801
Dr Maclaine comes to me to-morrow to meet the Bishop of Killala whose letter is published with an account of his spirited behaviour when the French were at his house in Ireland   My good Dr Maclaine,

of age ; he used to laugh at my father for his nervousness, and tell him to look
in the glass and ask himself if he could have ought to complain of   Animated
by religious principles, and full of literary pursuit, as Paley describes, on the
edge of two worlds, Dr. Maclaine enjoyed the present life in reality, and the
future in anticipation.

He took pleasure in my father's society, who continually visited him, and
through Miss Maclaine was introduced, after the death of her father, to Lady
Hesketh,[1] the cousin of Cowper.

At Bath he also became acquainted with the two Duncans,[2] men whose
principles were liberal as his own, and whose lives are devoted to the happiness
of their fellow-beings, whilst they cultivate those tastes and talents which add
so much to the charm of society, and in many instances are productive—in
hands like theirs—of still more good than the obvious modes of accomplishing it.

The warm and unvarying affection of these brothers for each other,
particularly recommended them to a family like ours, drawing so much of its
happiness from domestic life.

---

alas ! looks declining, and reminds me but too much of his being eighty years old   Yet at times his fire
and spirit are still alive   One evening he and the Wilberforces drank tea with me, and the conversation
was so lively pleasant, I never thought of age in the good old man

Letter from the same to the same   Barley Wood, July 22nd, 1802 —" From the house of Hannah
More, I had made an agreement with H More to pass a week with her, and I came yesterday, when I
parted with my dear Sir Thomas Rivers, who was a fortnight at Bath   It is credibly reported that we were
seven hours *tête-a-tête* and greatly surprised when, forgetting supper, we heard the clock strike eleven !
The worst of this indiscretion is that my poor Dr Maclaine is terribly jealous, and very unhappy about it ,
luckily the rival is removed ! "

[1] Note as to Lady Hesketh from Mrs Johnson's " Letters of Lady Hesketh," Jarrold, Norwich, 1901.

Lady Hesketh, wife of Sir Thomas Hesketh, was first cousin to Cowper, and sister of his early
love, Theodora   Both were daughters of Mr Ashley Cowper, whose house in Southampton Row,
became a home to Cowper, when at eighteen years of age, he was articled to a solicitor in London
for three years   Lady Hesketh did not become a regular correspondent of Cowper's until twenty
years after he left London, *viz*, October, 1792, but from that time till his death they wrote to
each other frequently   Her own health and nerves were shattered by the strain of attending him at
Weston Underwood   Lady Hesketh died on January 15th, 1807

[2] Philip Bury Duncan, D C L (1772-1863), Keeper of the Ashmolean Museum at Oxford   Established at Bath and Oxford a Savings Bank and Society for suppression of mendicity   John Shute
Duncan, brother of the above, was Keeper of Ashmolean Museum until 1826, when his brother
succeeded him.

PLATE XIII

KEY TO THE PREVIOUS PLATE

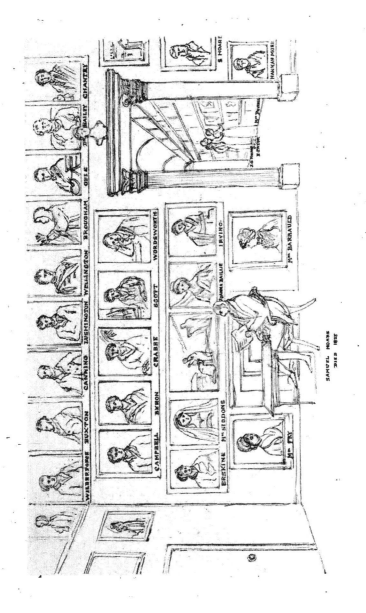

Our friendship with Mr. Milford led to the marriage of his only daughter, Mary, with my cousin, George Kett,[1] and a union thus brought about, was a source of pleasure to my father, particularly as she was always a favourite with him, and has ever proved her value for this preference.

At Bath he was consulted as an oracle by persons who wanted advice about their affairs, and in his political speculations he was remarkably true ; and, though sometimes standing alone, events have sometimes justified his opinions

We were spared from all panics   He never feared invasion, never talked of burying money, or securing it in foreign funds , never, in temporary disturbances, suspected that the mob would be long triumphant ; never thought the country would be starved, or the existing order of things overturned , and always believed that good would prevail over evil in this country

His old friend Mr. Wilberforce,[2] said, one day, that he would treat him as a certain fish, which its sick brothers rubbed themselves against for the cure of their infirmities, and thus get rid of political despondency.

The cheerfulness of his voice and manner, and the remarkable degree of sympathy he felt for the sick and unfortunate, made his visits delightful, and orders were frequently given to let him in at any hour, though others were excluded. His knock and ring were signals of pleasure—I do not exaggerate—, and I am sure he exemplified one line of his favourite song, " His very step hath music in it when he comes up the stair."[3]

He took interest in trifles, rode fine horses, enjoyed playing chess and billiards, and forgot for a time he was an invalid, and had so little the countenance and voice of suffering, that the inexperienced could scarcely believe that he knew it but by name.

At Bath I asked and obtained his permission to become a member of the Church of England, but as I was out of health and spirits, he strongly advised

[1] Of Brooke House, Norfolk

[2] William Wilberforce (1759-1833), M P for Hull. Leader of the abolition movement in Parliament.

[3] From the song " There's nae luck about the house " or the Mariner's Wife, by W J Mickle, (1734-1788).

me to wait one year, as it had always been his rule to make no important change
of any kind whilst the feelings were under painful impressions , and that in cases
where delay is possible, it is wisdom to wait till they have assumed their
accustomed tone

The sacraments of baptism and the Lord's supper he considered but as
forms ; and though they might be means of grace, the shadows were unimportant
if the substance can be obtained without them   But he wished everyone to
follow the bent of their own minds   He decidedly preferred the Church of
England to Dissenters of any description, with the exception of Friends ; and
continually went to Church, but without joining in the whole of the worship.
His creed was less defined than those of the Church   To that of St. Athanasius
he greatly objected, often absenting himself from Church when it was read, and
asking people how they could think of condemning him by repeating it

Though educated in a Society which does not dwell much upon points of
doctrine, independent of its peculiar views, he was a believer in the three Persons
of the Trinity, in the miraculous birth of Christ the Son of God and in the influence
of the Holy Spirit.   The Atonement he considered a mystery beyond the compre-
hension of man, but that the death of Christ was equal to the sin of Adam.
" That as in Adam all die, even so in Christ shall all be made alive."   This text
he thought against the eternity of punishment, and was indisposed to believe
that a being, whose sins could only be finite, would be everlastingly punished
by a beneficent Being, who created man for his own happiness, and is incapable
of wrath and revenge ; words only used in Scripture to denote His disapprobation of sin.

He never spoke harshly of differences in religious opinion, holding that
every man who sought truth, would find sufficient for his own salvation, however
he might dissent from the creeds of others

He objected to the errors of Socinians, still more to the narrow views of
Calvin, which accuse the Almighty of creating man for destruction, and quoted
a sentiment of John Wesley, " That this is ascribing to the Author of good a
work with which devils have never been charged."

One afternoon he said to a clergyman, whose liberality he suspected, " F——, I sent my groom to North Walsham on horse-back without directing him the right way, and after the poor fellow had done his best to find it (but in vain), I commanded him to be punished   Do you not think me a very cruel master ? What can you think of God, who thus deals,—you say—with His creatures ? "

To Mrs C——, who said one day to him that she was nothing but a mass of sin, he said, " Then I am afraid to come near you ! "

He fully admitted the two principles spoken of by St Paul, the evil struggling against the good ; and reprobated the idea of merit : " What hast thou that thou didst not receive ? " but never believed there was a time when the evil existed in us without the counteracting good

All that is important in the Christian religion he looked upon as perfectly simple. " The wayfaring man cannot err therein , earnest endeavour must meet with success ; people trouble themselves uselessly about faith and works ; the one is the principle, the other its result."

The view taken by the narrow-minded of the state of heathens was abhorrent to his enlarged mind ; and whatever his regard might be for individuals, he ever spoke with dislike of their opinions

Such was his love of God, that he never feared evil at His hand, perfectly resigned to His will in sickness and health, sorrow and joy. Persuaded that He who created man must be infinitely wiser than the work of His hand, knowing far better what is for his true good, he latterly never experienced the pains connected with religion, possessing we humbly trust, through life and in death, " the peace which passeth all understanding."

Though I was the first of my family who desired to join the Church, I was not the first to make this change, for my youngest sister, Sophia, took this important step previous to her marriage with Mr. Powell, of Loughton, August 10th, 1811.[1]

My father consented to this marriage, though by no means blinded by his own to the two-fold disadvantage,—of great inequality of age between the parties, and a family of children by a former wife.

[1] The date of this marriage was 9th August, 1810, not as stated here

Sophy was eight and twenty, and consequently permitted more liberty of judging for herself than if she had been a younger woman   Nothing could have been more ungenerous than for any of us to have deceived or disobeyed such a father, for he never concealed from us that if we had acted contrary to his wishes he would have forgiven us, making the best of what was inevitable, and restoring us to favour and peace.   Indeed no one could have more earnestly promoted domestic harmony, or set a more powerful example of it, even under circumstances which would have been highly irritating to other men

Two events took place in 1815 which secured to our family two friends who have been a source of more interest to my father and mother and myself than almost any we before possessed   The one was in the autumn when the daughter of our old friend Mrs. Lloyd died in her confinement.   She had been eleven years the wife of Dr. Wordsworth,[1] and he, knowing her attachment to our family, particularly to my mother, so constantly applied to her for help and advice respecting his three sons, and they all spent so much time with us at Hampstead, that more than the usual interest of relationship has been established amongst us

The other circumstance was an introduction to Mr. Crabbe,[2] with whom we were not immediately pleased.   He was, however, sufficiently attracted by us to induce him to take great pains to gain my father, and, in the end, so completely succeeded that I think no person out of his own family gave him equal enjoyment.   They would talk of public characters and political events which took place before my existence, and could sympathize with each other in the infirmities of advancing age.   Mr. Crabbe's poetry had been highly amusing to my father long before he became acquainted with its author.   His letters to me were destined to amuse some of the last hours of the life of his friend.   Their minds were on many points congenial, each thinking for himself, unenslaved by the opinions of others, and, exercising strong understandings in the most important subjects connected with our existence, they continually came to the same conclusions.

[1] See note ante on p 27
[2] The Rev George Crabbe (1754-1832), the poet.

Grizell Hoare.
(*wife of David Powell of Loughton*)

Graves, Windsor Ph. sc.

My father shared the common hopes and fears of his country in the peace made with France, 1814; the escape of Napoleon; and the battle of Waterloo.

Trusting in the superiority of our navy, and calculating the length of time which must elapse before a fleet could be raised, he never believed it possible that Buonaparte would make good a landing in this country.

Educated in the principles of a sect reprobating war, he looked upon it, in the present state of society, as a necessary evil Defensive war he regarded as lawful ; the nice point was determined when it became so ; for where preventive measures are not had recourse to, defence may become impracticable.

He quoted the text, " Whoso sheddeth man's blood, by man shall his blood be shed, " He applied it to capital punishment

Self-defence he considered lawful, and that it is the duty of a man to defend his family

It was not the habit of his mind to give hastily in to new systems He was not a projector of the improvement of prison discipline. He encouraged by subscriptions and had great personal attachment to Elizabeth Fry.

The Bills brought forward in the House of Commons for the final abolition of slavery he did not completely coincide with , he questioned the possibility of the measure, and thought the honour of the country too far pledged to the planters to withdraw her protection.

New companies and speculations he usually disapproved, and never looked with the same complacency upon fortunes acquired by their means as in the steady course of business.

He was peculiarly prosperous in his own money transactions, indeed very early in life he was considered a fortunate man ; so much so, that a gentleman whom he knew desired him to buy with his own hand lottery tickets for good luck. The first of these tickets drawn turned up a £20 prize , and writing to congratulate the man on his good fortune, he said he hoped shortly to add two additional cyphers. The next ticket literally fulfilled this hope, and the man, delighted with his £2,000, presented him with a gold watch which has been his constant companion through life, always going correctly, but lately become so battered and out of repair, that I did not like to look at it.

Two deaths occurred in his family which excited very different sensations,—that of my aunt Mary Hoare, and that of my uncle Jonathan. She had been his favourite sister, and, with many peculiarities was a good and sensible woman. She had a cancerous knot in her breast five months before it was thought necessary to submit to amputation. She was anxious to conceal the circumstances till the operation had taken place, knowing the pain it would give my father. Nothing unfavourable appeared during the amputation, and for some days after the wound was healing　But her constitution was not strong enough to bear so great a shock, and she peacefully expired in the winter of 1819, conscious of her end, and speaking of the calmness in which she had been preserved

My uncle Jonathan¹ died 1820, and my uncle Kett (who had been far more than a brother to my father, and with whom he lived on a footing of great intimacy) in the same year.

A far heavier blow awaited him in the death [March, 1821] of my brother-in-law Pryor,—cut off in the prime of life, and leaving my sister a widow with five children　He died in full confidence that her father, whom he loved and revered, would be a second father to them, and so, I am sure, he proved, thinking no trifle in which their interests were concerned beneath his notice, obviating every difficulty which arose in my sister's desolate circumstances, and for years never liking to be absent from her many weeks together.

He was prepared for this sad event by poor Pryor having been struck with apoplexy the preceding summer , but felt it so much when it actually took place, that we dreaded the effect it might have on his own health.

I rejoiced that he stayed at Bath a few weeks after receiving the last account, in some degree to recruit his spirits and to give us time to compose ourselves a little before he came amongst us.

¹ Jonathan Hoare's death occurred in 1819, the year before that of Thos Kett, of Seething

.

Thomas Marlborough Pryor

Emery Walker Ph. Sc.

He had himself been dangerously ill with cramp and a bilious affection the preceding autumn ; and from that period began to grow thin, and lost some strength. Still he had an unusual portion for his time of life

In the summer and autumn of 1824 his breath was occasionally affected walking up hill, though he was tolerably well at Cromer, and daily mounted the cliff from the jetty. For several years he had given up shooting, but enjoyed riding on horseback, and witnessing the exploits of my brother and his boys.

In January, 1825, after dinner at my sister Pryor's, my father awoke from a short sleep confused in his mind. We were much alarmed, but as he soon recovered himself, considered the ill only an affection of the stomach, and proceeded to Bath the next day, as we had previously intended

He bore the journey better than usual, and met his old friends with pleasure, —Mr. Lloyd, the Warners, and Mrs Hughan and her sister Justina,[1] who came to spend a week with him.

He visited Priscilla Gurney[2] in her chamber, admiring her saint-like beauty and character.

Mr. Crabbe was much with him, and the last long walk he ever took was to see the Duncans.

Billiards and chess went on as usual ; and he read with great interest of an evening Prior's " Life of Burke "

His breathing became worse the day before we set out for home, and he was unusually nervous on the journey. His feet and ankles had been swelled for some weeks, but, for a short time after our return, were nearly their usual size We were uneasy. He had a bad cold, which increased the oppression on his breath ; and about mid-Lent, coming from church, Mr. Haines's manner made me fearful. Still it was not till Easter that I became acutely anxious, and the following week he had an attack of sickness which was succeeded by frequent attacks on the same kind ; and though Dr. Luke was called in, and assured us

[1] Justina Milligan and Charles Sterry, Deputy Master of the Mint, were great friends

[2] Priscilla Hannah Gurney, daughter of Joseph Gurney and Christiana Barclay, his wife, granddaughter of Robt Barclay the apologist —[Cf " Gurneys of Earlham," I , 302-303]

that his patient was free from actual disease, the anxiety I suffered was beyond anything I can, or ought to, describe here.

The sickness was stopped, apparently, by small quantities of potash about five weeks after its commencement, when we began to hope all might be yet well But this hope was short. Symptoms of dropsy and general decline pressed heavily upon us Dr Luke pronounced the disease to be water on the chest, and Dr. Babbington was called in for a consultation Both physicians pressed upon us the necessity of appearing cheerful, as the least alarm my father might feel on his own account would probably prove instantly fatal; and a merciful God enabled us to banish our heartfelt wretchedness, both from our looks and manner.

Notwithstanding the frequent returns of spasms on the breath, he was able to drive my mother in the pony-cart, and was at chapel on the 4th of July. I think he had rode on horse-back the preceding Sunday. On the 5th he became much worse, and suffered for hours every morning with the oppression and spasmodic affection on his breath. He afterwards liked to be read to, and played chess with interest.

On the 11th he slept in the drawing-room,'which he had prepared for him, that he might not suffer from walking upstairs. He was pleased with the change, and with almost everything that was done for him Nothing could exceed his patience, and we think he did not speak to us as though he knew his end was approaching, lest it should be over-setting to us, and perhaps to himself.

For the last three days he kept his bed, and my mother never left him. The sight of his suffering from the spasms subdued all human fortitude, but there was a Divine arm supporting both him and us We have reason to believe that the Almighty, whom he had loved in prosperity, made " all his bed in sickness."

On Thursday at eleven in the morning, he breathed his last, and expired without a struggle. The Wednesday following he was buried at Winchmore Hill in the same grave with my mother.

' To make the room convenient for the invalid, a fine six fold Oriental screen was purchased This is now at Catton.

PLATE XVI.

PORTRAIT OF SARAH HOARE (1777-1856)

From the drawing by Josiah Slater, at Weston

Sarah Hoare

Josiah Slater Del.

Emery Walker Ph. Sc.

My brother only attended of his children, but there were many relations and friends present at the funeral, with eyes steeped in tears, and hearts heavy with grief.

Mrs. Chorley[1] who was there said, " Others wept, but I could shed no tear I considered that he who has been my friend for fifty years, is only separated from me for a short space to receive me into mansions of eternal joy ! "

Shops were voluntarily shut up at Hampstead, and every demonstration of grief given on this sad occasion, both by rich and poor.

Sir Wm. Pepys[2] said on only seeing his picture, " You have that in your countenance which I would fain call master " ; and the expression of the Italian poet might be justly applied to him, " Natura il fece, e poi ruppe la stampa."

Were I to describe his distinguishing feature, I should say it was true nobility of character, above the pursuits of ambition Nothing appeared to him great, but what was good. He scorned the petty distinctions upon which others prided themselves, and the arts by which they obtained them ; delighting only in power, because it enabled him to gratify the unbounded benevolence of his nature

He gave liberally as he would pay a debt, and never called this a virtue.

All who were associated with him, treated him with instinctive reverence, unmixed with fear, for he exacted nothing.

His grandchildren delighted in him ; the younger ones were his playthings ; and he loved those who were old enough to be his companions with almost paternal tenderness.

The God whom he served had stamped so much holiness on his nature, that he called forth in others some of the best feelings and affections of which they were capable No one had more sincere friends without a single enemy.

He could reprove without offending because he affected no superiority, and was ever careful first to " hear, then examine, then rebuke," and ventured to expostulate with others on occasions in which no one else would have interfered. His cautions and warnings were ever well received

[1] She was then in her eightieth year

[2] W Weller Pepys, one of the masters in the High Court of Chancery, created Baronet 1801, died 1825

He was careful to keep up the ties of relationship and family connection, and to fulfil the precept, "Thine own friend and thy father's friend forsake not!"

He loved a cheerful countenance, and quoted a passage from Tillotson, "that in our pursuit of heaven, we must not forget that we have to live upon earth"

Sorrowful it is to reflect how little of what he was can be preserved by the pen or the pencil   To those who have known him from their infancy, lived with him, and delighted in him, no outward remembrances are required ; deeply are they engraved upon the heart by the finger of "love strong as death." To those who but imperfectly recollect him, this memoir may be of value.   If they be his descendants, and inherit from him some portion of the right feeling which distinguished him, they will prize far beyond any adventitious honours the privilege of having sprung from such an ancestor, and emulate the virtues which exalted him above his fellow beings, and the humility which was conspicuous above them all,—not charging himself with sins he had never committed, or depravity which he did not feel, but saying with St Paul, "What hast thou that thou didst not receive ?"

PLATE XVII.

SILHOUETTE OF J. GURNEY HOARE, APRIL 1820,

From Hannah Hoare's Profile-book.

Gurney Hoare
April 1820

Henry Walton Phot.

Samuel Hinkes
April 1820

Mrs Joanna Baillie
(1820)

Mrs Schimmelpenninck
(1809)

14

Mrs Galton
(Lucy Barclay of Ury)

Sophia Bland

Engraved by Walter Pen Sc.

John Pryor of Baldock.

Emery Walker Ph. Sc

Stuarton pinxit.

Hannah Sterry
(2nd wife of Samuel Hoare)

Emery Walker Ph.sc.

A MEMOIR OF SAMUEL HOARE.
BY HANNAH HOARE, HIS WIDOW.
WRITTEN IN AUGUST, MDCCCXXV.

With the earnest desire that my memory may preserve the dearest treasure committed to its trust, I now endeavour to retrace some of the circumstances in the life of my most tenderly beloved husband, "but let not the excess of love and delight in the stream, make me forget the fountain   He and all his excellences come from God and flowed back into their own spring : there let me seek them, thither let me hasten after him.   There having found him, let me cease to bewail among the dead that which is risen."

He was born in the first house in Paradise Row, Stoke Newington, on the 9th of August, 1751 ; his father, Samuel Hoare, was of an Irish family, one of five sons, who all embraced different religious opinions, his Mother, Grizell Gurnell, was of a wealthy family living at Ealing, a village in the neighbourhood of London.   My husband was the fifth child of this marriage, the two first died in infancy, the third a daughter survived, and the fourth a son named Joseph lived to manhood and then died in consumption.   There were, besides these, one son and three daughters who all lived beyond the middle period of life, making in all the whole nine children.

When Samuel, the subject of this memoir, was five years old, he was sent with his elder brother Joseph to a school at Penketh in Lancashire, and was taken home only once in the year for vacation ; he was of a robust constitution, with great tenderness of mind, which made him seriously feel any deviation

from truth, or any instances in which he had been carelessly guilty of cruelty
to animals   At about twelve years of age he was sent to a seminary for education under John Riveaux, in the Grange Road, and at fourteen he was apprenticed to Henry Gurney at Norwich, to learn the trade of a Norwich manufacturer,
where he continued till he was twenty-one   At this period he was deeply and
strongly imbued with religious sentiments in conformity with the Society of
Friends, of which his family and himself were members, and he was deputed
to attend their Yearly Meeting in London when his apprenticeship expired :
a remarkable testimony to the stability and excellence of his conduct   I believe
that the conclusion his mind reached at this early period of his life upon the
great doctrines of religion remained unshaken, and that as he made Christianity
in its most extensive and exalted character the guide of his youth, so did it
continue to support and comfort him through all the remaining stages of his
existence, and knowing in whom he believed, the stay to his mind was so
firmly established that it became its habitual bias.   About this time he wrote
some excellent rules for his conduct, to the substance of which he adhered with
conscientious strictness.

During his apprenticeship in Norwich, he formed some very valuable friendships which continued through life, helping to sweeten and cheer its progress.
In 1772 he was made a partner in the Banking House in Lombard Street, in
which he continued till the year 1825.   Here his temper was in the beginning
severely tried by the violence of one in the firm, and in struggling to overcome
the temptation to retaliate, he gained a command over himself which he never
afterwards lost

At this period it was convenient to him to have apartments in London, as
his father's family continued to reside at Newington, and he lodged and boarded
in the house of John and Alice Chorley   He formed a strong and very intimate
friendship with the latter, her powerful understanding and enthusiasm for his
character excited a great degree of admiration and esteem in him, combined with
strong affection which under a lower standard of religious principle might have
tended to undermine happiness   In this interval his taste for literature was

strengthened, he read with her and was associated with men of talent who frequented her house   At the age of twenty-five, on the 15th of May, 1776, he married Sarah Gurney, of Norwich ; she was in her nineteenth year, of a sweet temper and gentle manners, with tender spirits and of strong affections ; the expression of her countenance was pleasing and intellectual but not handsome ; with her he enjoyed a rich share of happiness, but it was of short duration   She died on the 31st of January, 1783, in the fourth lying in, leaving him with three girls and the infant boy , he had delighted in the birth of a son and said that his happiness was too great in the event of peace with America and the blessing of his child   Her death, which was sudden, plunged him into the deepest sorrow, and the shock it produced upon his feelings he never completely recovered ; she had only said " I am faint," sank back and gradually died   His two sisters were with him alternately in Broad Street till the spring, when he removed with his children to a small house in Paradise Row close to his father's , one of his unmarried sisters used to breakfast with him daily, and he spent his evenings in their family circle   In 1786 he went into a larger house in the same Row, and in about three years from the time of his wife's death he began to think of marrying again   Although I was not then seventeen years old, there was a feeling of affection inspired, which gradually grew in both our hearts, and united us in the closest and tenderest bonds on the 17th of June, 1788   My own family objected to this marriage as ineligible for so young a woman.   My husband was thirty-six years old, tall, of dignified, benevolent manners, handsome and possessing every requisite to please and gratify the taste and affections, as well as to excite a feeling of pride and self-complacency in being the object of his choice.   With so wise and able a counsellor to whom I looked up with great veneration, as well as love, my character became formed ; and few, very few, were my pains and trials compared with the portion of happiness I now enjoyed, and I believe we were at this early period made a blessing to each other, whilst the high sense I entertained of the duty of a wife to him, and that of a mother to his children, established feelings and principles which strengthened with my increasing years.   Having no family of my own was a source of sorrow and disappointment, which continued for nearly twenty years, but my husband, wiser than I, had no regrets, knowing how often the difficulties arising from two families, interfere with happiness   I constantly guarded against betraying my feelings, lest I should blast the enjoyment I had in his children by showing them that they could not fully satisfy me, and their affection for me was so strong, that I believe they could not have loved me better if I had been really their mother   Still I had many a hard struggle with myself, till about the year 1800, when a strong and deep religious influence enabled me to submit to this dispensation as wisely ordered by my Heavenly Father " whose ways are not as our ways," and from this time the bitterness of the trial was overcome.

A very heavy affliction was appointed us in less than two years after our marriage in the severe nervous illness of my husband.   He had been attacked in the same manner before, but to me the alarm and anxiety were very great, he often thought himself dying, and lost his strength and flesh with very distressing sensations arising from nervous depression.   In the winter of 1789 we went to Bath by the advice of his physicians, where he gradually recovered, and by their advice also in June, 1790, we removed from Newington to Hampstead Heath as a higher and drier situation   This change was productive of great comfort and benefit, as it set me at liberty to act with more freedom, and independence than I could do so immediately under the inspection of my husband's family, from whom I received very great kindness, but there was a degree of roughness and decision in their manners, overpowering to the timidity attendant on my youth, and natural character, which kept my mind back and was a disadvantage to the children   At this time the tie of affection which subsisted between our family and that of my husband's first wife, was generously and greatly strengthened, and I remember their love for me amongst my choicest blessings.   It was a rare instance of generosity and kindness on their part, and of discretion from my husband's wise guidance on ours.

In 1796 his father died.   He was a man of remarkable clearness and firmness of mind, just in discriminating and concise in his mode of expression ; of great singularity of manner and almost a slave to habit ; he dressed in the

Hannah Pryor
1818

Emery, Whitmore

style of 1748 and lived completely by rule   He was a Friend in his religious
views, but did not unite in their peculiarities   The pain of the event of his
death was greatly mitigated from the feeble state both of body and mind which
he had been in for many months previously   The death of his mother, in 1802
my husband acutely felt, as his mother he loved her with the tenderness she
merited, for she was unbounded in kindness and affection to all around her.   I
think it was about this juncture, my anxiety grew so great, from the repeated
attacks of nervous illness, that I privately consulted Dr. Sims upon the great
irregularity of pulse.   He and other physicians seemed to treat it lightly, but
perhaps this was from knowing that it arose from some latent affection connected
with the heart, which it was not in human skill to rectify, and which I believe
increased with years, and finally arrested the vital powers.

Our dear daughter Hannah married in 1802, an event fraught with great
comfort ;   her father with his habitual kindness exerted himself and succeeded
in finding a suitable house for her in Hampstead, and the affection which her
husband's sweetness of character justly inspired, and her increasing family, were
new sources of happiness to us both   Our son's marriage in 1806 was delightful
to his father, and the pleasures of his living close by our home, and having the
children immediately about him, constituted some of his brightest enjoyment
Our youngest daughter married in 1810, under circumstances which her father
thought ineligible, but he yielded to her wishes with the greatest kindness and
generosity.   From these marriages we were blest with nineteen grandchildren,
but the loss of our dear Hannah's husband in 1821 was a very great blight to our
family happiness.

Nervous illness and great depression arising from this source were the
important drawbacks to our comfort and enjoyment, and my husband used often
to say that if it were not for this trial he should be too happy, but with this
constant check upon all our projects and the experience we dearly bought in
the few journeys we made for pleasure, our habits gradually grew into the
regular system, and as Bath was a place which suited him, from its waters and
also from the opportunity it afforded for social enjoyment without the form

of engagements, we went there almost every winter for about two months, and in the month of September we as regularly went to Cromer, where we had a house and small estate. Here he had very great enjoyment in shooting, till the year 1820, when his health no longer allowed him to take the exercise without great fatigue, but I never heard him murmur or repine; he used to speak of the inroads time made upon the frame as a common event, and seemed able to substitute one pleasure as another was withdrawn, and the afternoons were usually given to drive out with me, with the variety of playing at billiards for a few hours occasionally. I think the time we spent in Norfolk was generally the brightest portion of the year, he was known to every person in the town of Cromer, and as universally beloved, for he was truly the friend and comforter of all who surrounded him

During the last ten years we seldom dined out, or had any set company, but we kept up a close intercourse with our family and most intimate friends; and had always pleasant and good society, which he completely enjoyed, when he was tolerably well, and would with great kindness and benevolence accommodate himself to those whose manners were least agreeable, never suffering difference in religious opinion, which did not affect moral character, to prevent his serving those people who wanted help and advice To the poor he was tender and compassionate, and to those who were removed from indigence soothing and affectionate, often calling upon them, when he thought he could cheer or amuse them under affliction or aid them by his counsel, so that it might be said of him as of his great Pattern " he went about doing good " He used to play at billiards, for exercise and amusement, and at chess with great interest, and was so zealous in the game that it often beguiled a nervous hour when other resources failed.

In the sleepless nights attending upon his illness I used often to read to him, and this habit continued at intervals for many years, till my eyes became affected and compelled me reluctantly to give it up Cowper's letters and poems, Johnson's Life, Wordsworth's biography, with books of the same class amused and pleased him; he generally read daily in the Scriptures; Wilson's "Sacra Privata," Kempis's "Imitation of Christ " and Law's "Serious Call," were

Mrs. Samuel Hoare   Sarah Hoare   Samuel Hoare

Emery Walker Ph.Sc.

amongst his favourite religious books, and he used often to say that a few pages well read and thought upon were of much more real benefit to the mind, than many long sermons Porteus' sermon on Contentment, and Tillotson's on Sincerity both suited his feelings, and I read the former so often when he was particularly poorly, that I know many passages of it by heart

In the Spring of 1825, his constitution indicated important change and seemed to be giving way, his breath was at times oppressed in walking up hill, still I did not believe the affliction so near that was in store for me, and not till the 24th of June when our medical friend thought it right to apprise me of it, did I imagine danger very near, though my heart had been very sad and anxious for many months The 14th of July, 1825, terminated the period of my earthly happiness ; though I trust not of peace and submissive resignation. After having spent thirty-seven years in a dependence so close, that we were never separated but once for two days, it is natural that all my habits should have been those which are created by the strongest and tenderest affection, and that the breaking of such a tie should be like that of terminating my existence, as it relates to the spirits, objects and business of life, for it throws me wholly into a new sphere or rather casts me into the current, without any outward pilot on the ocean of life.

But for the years that are past let me be thankful and patiently wait the Lord's will till my change come, and if those years or days which are yet to come be the means of fitting me for a reunion with him who was so infinitely dear to me, I bless and praise my God, for this added portion, however long and bitter may be the duration, trusting that He will, amidst the dreariness of my earthly pilgrimage, point out the path of duty and with his staff support me in it and by the light of his countenance guide me to those heavenly regions where sorrow and sighing will cease for ever. To all his family my dearest husband was truly tender and affectionate, to me an entire union of heart with the utmost and unbounded confidence that excused all my failings and gave me credit for unlimited love and devotedness to himself. Our days passed in mutual depend-ence and if I could be with him he often and constantly said he was quite

satisfied and wanted no other society.   We used often to read together, but from
the constant watchfulness which I practised I never read passages which I
thought would give him pain, and avoided all details of death as a subject alive
in both our minds, but we did not speak upon it except that by allusion he
sometimes said I was like a miser who loved his treasure the better as he was
nearer losing it, and I did not speak of the future in the later few months lest
it should draw forth a painful feeling   He was carefully considerate of the
feelings of others and used to caution me from hasty judgments by saying " first
hear, then examine, then rebuke " , towards himself he was strict in the perform-
ance of duties—patience and submission to the Divine Will were his marked
characteristics, and he used to say that people hurt both their tempers and their
faith by discussing controversial points in doctrine, which were beyond the
reach of human wisdom.   He often quoted William Penn's letter to Archbishop
Tillotson where he says " I abhor two principles in religion and pity those who
hold them   The first is obedience upon authority without conviction, and the
other destroying those who differ from me for God's sake."   Of social duties
he had a high sense, quoting Tillotson's sentiment " that in fixing our eyes upon
Heaven we ought not to forget that we have our part to perform upon earth."

He loved a cheerful spirit and that religion should shine forth in the daily
routine of life, by its fruit of love and good will, saying he liked sweetness mixed
with gravity and cheerfulness tempered with sobriety.

His countenance was so true an index of his mind that when Sir W. Pepys
saw a sketch of him by Slater, he at once applied the passage from Shakespeare,
" There is something in that man's face I would fain call master," and his manner
equally denoted the benevolence and charity of his heart, which the Rev. Mr.
Morgan beautifully describes from a short interview, to beg money to assist a school
for the poor.   He says in a letter to a friend " I was truly grieved to notice
the death of Mr. Hoare in the day's paper—I never spoke to him but once, and
then he manifested the greatest degree of Christian sympathy and brotherly
love and kindness, that I ever witnessed in anyone, he so entirely won my heart
that I really loved him with as much sincerity as if he had been my father."

PLATE XXVII

PORTRAIT OF HANNAH STERRY, SECOND WIFE OF SAMUEL HOARE

From a drawing in pastels, at Weston

.

Hannah Sterry
(2nd wife of Samuel Hoare)

May I be permitted patiently to wait, and may I mercifully be allowed the cheering hope that in the Lord's good time I shall be blest with him, who was my treasure upon earth, in those Heavenly Mansions whereinto he is already entered, I trust his spirit is waiting to receive mine, amidst those who are favoured to inherit eternal life.

HANNAH HOARE.

Autumn, 1825

LETTERS WRITTEN AT THE TIME OF THE GORDON RIOTS
BY SARAH HOARE, FIRST WIFE OF THE SUBJECT OF THESE
MEMOIRS, TO HER MOTHER, MRS BLAND, AT NORWICH.

Broad Street,

6th month, 2d, 1780.

Sincerely do I hope, my dearest Mother, that these lines will find thee. I congratulate thee on my Father's 'safe return, and that the long period of absence which have been so painful may at length be terminated. I please myself with the idea that thou wilt think he looks well, and if you are favoured with good health it will greatly increase your mutual satisfaction, in which I trust all your children will abundantly participate

It is not half-an-hour since thy acceptable line reached my hand. I had all day intended to converse with thee this evening, when the receipt of thine determined me to put it in immediate execution.

I rejoice to hear that my brother and sister Kett are comfortably settled in their own habitation, where I doubt not but they enjoy as much happiness as reciprocal affection and friendship can bestow. I am concerned for their perplexity about the carpets, as it would be an awkward circumstance to be prevented seeing their company before yearly meeting, but I own, that as Moore is concerned in sending them, I am apprehensive they will be disappointed, for from troublesome experience, I can certify to the tedious manner in which he executes commissions

My father Hoare saw Dr Fothergill, and Surgeon Potts yesterday, who were both of opinion that Scarborough will be of service to him, and recommend him

---

¹ Thomas Bland was step-father to the writer   [E T]

54

to go by easy stages, in about three weeks, if he continues as well as he is now. We all are pleased they think him well enough to undertake the journey, altho' to those who are left behind, I am persuaded it will prove a time of painful solicitude

As my brother Bradshaw has business which will call him very soon to Ireland, I believe my sister and the children will accompany my Father to Scarborough, which will make it more cheerful for my sisters. I am sorry to say that Polly¹ is very poorly.

Every one is anxious to hear the conclusion of an affair which has made great noise in the city all this day. Thou hast most probably heard of the meeting which was advertised to be held in George's Fields, to proceed from thence in procession to the House of Commons, to deliver a petition from the Protestants Accordingly fifty thousand men divided into companys of eight-thousand each, with Lord George Gordon at their head, assembled at the hour appointed, and marched through the City. The Guards were ordered out, and many feared that would produce great confusion. What reception they met with on their arrival I have not heard I must own I have seldom felt my fears equally awakened, and it is to this circumstance thou must ascribe the trouble of reading this narration, for had not this been the case, I think I should not have introduced politicks into my letter ; but I am so much accustomed to communicate with thee whatever gives me either pain, or pleasure, that I could not well resist the temptation.

My Samuel and dear girls,² are quite well. The warmth of the weather rather fatigues the children, and we are glad to find them amusement within doors, to prevent their being desirous of going out.

My dearest companion unites with me in the salutation of unfeigned affection to all your circle while I subscribe myself [thy] sincerely dutiful and affectionate daughter.

S. HOARE.

¹ Mary Hoare, her sister-in-law
² Sarah and Hannah Hoare, born 1777 and 1779

17

Fourth day, evening.

MY DEAREST MOTHER,

The agitation of my mind at the present moment is such as I fear will prevent writing intelligible , but as I know thou wilt be rejoiced to hear of our welfare, I am unwilling not to attempt giving thee this comfortable intelligence.

I doubt not the accounts of the alarming riots which have disturbed the city for several days, have reached you ere now.

Ever since I last wrote thee, we have been kept in continual apprehensions The last three nights have presented scenes which my heart is ready to tremble at the remembrance of   We have each night seen dreadful fires burning,—but the last far exceeded the others.   Newgate was then destroyed, and every prisoner confined therein, set at liberty,   Lord Mansfield's house was also burned to the ground ; and the Guards opposing, seven of the mob were killed.   This has rendered them more desperate than before, and it is feared that this night will prove more dreadful than any preceding.   Whilst I write I am continually interrupted by small parties passing through the street, and the cry of " No Popery " is heard from every corner.

A large body of them are now assembled in Abchurch Lane, and are attempting to pull down a house ; but the Guards have hitherto prevented them from effecting their purpose.

Thy letter, dearest Mother, came most seasonably , I thank thee for it.   May I be enabled to adopt thy excellent council, and may it calm the painful temper which now disturbs my peace !   Do write me again very soon.   It will really be a comfort to me.   We are all favoured with good health.

There is now such a tumult in the street, that I cannot proceed.   Farewell ; most tenderly and most affectionately farewell.   Thyne sincerely,

S HOARE.

London, 5th day afternoon

MY DEAREST MOTHER,

The few lines which I hastily scribbled last night would, I fear, give thee much uneasiness from their abrupt conclusion. I have therefore again taken up my pen to tell thee how we are, and although this will prove the messenger of much melancholy tidings, yet, as our little circle are still favoured to enjoy health, and as much tranquility as the distressing situation of affairs will admit, I know it will be more satisfactory to you to hear, than that I should keep silent I had not finished my letter half an hour, when all was in confusion The mob attacked a house in Cushion Court, but were kept off by the Guards They then rushed forward to another [at] the corner of Wormwood Street, which they entered and stripped of everything which they could lay hold of, throwing them into the street, and setting them on fire on a large pile, which they kept constantly increasing.

This situation was dreadful beyond what I could form an idea of , but think how much the horror of this scene was heightened when a large party of the horse guards, attended by a company of volunteers, arrived They halted exactly opposite our house. Three times the commanding officer exhorted the people to disperse, but they obstinately refused. Then advancing but a few paces, they fired near a hundred pieces, and left four unhappy men dead on the spot, and fifteen wounded.

No words can describe our feelings at this moment ! Had it not been for my dearest Samuel's calmness and stability, I think I could scarcely have sustained the shock, but I believe we were both of us favoured with superior support and aid, and I have thankfully to acknowledge that I was still all the while

At the time this shocking affair happened, the King's Bench and Fleet prisons were both on fire, and burning with great fury, and another house in Houndsditch was in flames, that, from our windows, we beheld four dreadful conflagrations at one time.

About one in the morning all appeared quiet, and the fires extinguished We went upstairs to see our little girls, and rejoiced to find they had not been materially disturbed, and were sweetly asleep. But poor nurse, just as we entered, fell into a violent fit, and it was as much as we could do all of us to hold her for near an hour. This added to our distress, as it was impossible to send with safety for any assistance, as the city was put under Martial Law.

Soon after two we got her to bed, and as all seemed settled we went ourselves soon afterwards

My Father came and fetched the children and nurse down to Newington this morning. We were very glad to let him go for we are under some apprehension that two other houses in Broad Street will be served in like manner as that last night   I wish we may be mistaken.

It is said Lord Amherst, with all the troops which can be assembled, are to be in the City this evening at five o'clock   The gentlemen volunteer company are to join them, and every precaution is taken to prevent further mischief. Cannon is planted in several places   I ardently wish this may have the desired effect. Other ways it is feared that this night will be more dreadful than the last   I look forward to the approach of evening with sensations I cannot describe   I hope to write thee, my dearest Mother, better news to-morrow. Tell my beloved[1] sister, that as I have written thee, I conclude it the same as writing to her, and I could not do both. Do let me hear from you soon. Dear, dear love salutes your circle from my Samuel and thy sincerely affectionate daughter, S Hoare.

All well in Lombard Street.

----- - - -- - -

6th month, 9th, 1780

My Dearest Mother,

Thou wilt, I am certain, rejoice with us when I tell thee that peace is again restored. Last night a very large body of troops was stationed in different parts of the city, who patrolled the streets all night, and preserved *perfect* tranquillity. Not the least disturbance happened, and we have been favor'd to enjoy quiet all this day.

[1] Hannah, wife of Th Kett.

It is said not any appearance of mob have been seen, but all wears a hostile aspect. 300 soldiers are constantly on duty at the Excise Office, and guards are likewise placed at the Pay-office. The largest numbers are about the Bank, Post Office and Mansion House, that, should any further tumult arise, it is hoped they will be quickly quelled.

What a distressing alternative is this, yet it appeared the only one left.

The transactions of the last five days are, I believe, marked in indelible characters on our minds, and I hope we are truly thankful for the restoration of peace and tranquillity; indeed I cannot express what I felt, and do feel for the impressions still so strong upon my mind, that I tremble to look back, and am almost afraid to look forward. Ardently do I wish that we may ever remember the kind hand which has hitherto preserved us.

I am very anxious to hear of your welfare at Norwich, for as there have been reports of disturbances both at Manchester and Birmingham, we cannot help fearing for you also , I hope our fears are groundless

I had the satisfaction of hearing this morn'g that our dear girls are quite well, and their poor nurse better. I am expecting to take a ride in the evening to see them, which I shall be very glad of as I have not been out of the house since first day, excepting to meeting twice ; and my head begins to want a little air and exercise ; but for several days past it has been unsafe walking the streets alone, and the usual avenues out of town have been almost impassible towards evening.

It is an inexpressible comfort to me that my dearest companion has held well through all these distresses ; his company has been a constant support to me.

Uncle and Aunt Bland are well , poor Priscilla has been much alarmed and has been at Tottenham to be kept out of the way, as my aunt was fearful it might make an impression on her mind which could not easily be obliterated.

Accept thyself, my dearest Mother, and present to my Father and little Michael, the tenderest salutation of endeared love from my Samuel, and thy dutiful and affectionate daughter

S. HOARE.

The hurry in which I wrote my two last letters made me forget to mention that, in compliance with my dear sister's request I sent to enquire at Morrison's about the plate, and received for answer that it was sent to the Bull last third day week and I hope they have received it before now. I may add our dear love to this message, also love to Keziah Should everything remain quiet, I shall hardly write again before second day, but if not, thou may'st depend upon hearing.

[Letter from Samuel Hoare, Jr.]

FOR SARAH BLAND, AT THOMAS BLAND'S, NORWICH.

London, 10th June, 1780.

DEAR MOTHER,

I esteem myself much obliged by thy kind and affectionate remembrance in this time of trouble. We have great reason to be thankful that we have been quite clear of any mischief ourselves, tho' we have felt much anxiety on account of others

The firing so near our house, with the constant noise it occasioned, was a great exertion to my wife's spirits, but we seated ourselves quietly in the back-parlour, and she was more composed than could have been expected. She finds herself rather weak and languid owing to the fatigue, but I hope a few days quiet at Newington will set her perfectly well again

Our family have fixed their departure for next second day, for Scarborough. Many are suggesting suspicions and doubts in their minds respecting the cause of this tumult and one party reflecting on another as being instrumental ; but I apprehend one need not go deep for causes. The collection of such a large body together must consequentially bring many evil-minded persons together, and these would be ready enough at so fair an opportunity of doing mischief. So many abandoned wretches let out of Newgate must greatly increase the number.

We are now restored to peace thro' the assistance of Military Aid, but I think this would have been totally unnecessary had the Civil Magistrates done their duty at first.

Ld. G. Gordon was carried to the Tower last night.

Our babes are well, as is the family in Lombard Street.

Pray accept and distribute a large portion of our love as due from thy affectionate son, Saml Hoare, Jr.

Newington, 6th mo , 13th, 1780

MY DEAREST MOTHER,

Thou hast been kind indeed to remember us so frequently in our present state of anxiety, for although we are now favoured again to enjoy peace and tranquility, yet the recollection of what has passed have impressed us with such fear of the like in any future period, that I own I am afraid to look forward

I hope thou would not be made uneasy by our not writing thee yesterday, as my dearest Samuel requested my brother Kett to inform you of our welfare, and that we are comforted to find all remain quiet

My dear husband's letter on seventh day would inform thee of my being at Newington with our dear little children. I have thankfully to acknowledge that since I came here my mind have acquired much greater calmness than whilst I remained in London. Indeed I have been wonderfully supported throughout this distressing dispensation, far beyond what I could have expected ; and I trust my heart is filled with gratitude for this blessing

Our kind Father and Mother are desirous of our continuing here until fifth day, and we gladly accept their invitation. By that time I hope things will be in a more settled state, for while the City remains Martial Law, we are continually reminded of the dreadful necessity which produced it.

Sister Bradshaw and her little ones are also here. We expect our family to set off for Scarborough on second day. We are glad to see my Father on the whole is finely, and I think Polly is much better.

As I know it will be a satisfaction to you to hear frequently from us, I shall defer writing my dearest sister until to-morrow; had it not been for this consideration, I intended to have done it to-day. Pray give her and my dear brother my dear, dear love. My Hannah's [Mrs. Kett's] letter was truly comfortable to me. Indeed all your kind letters are more than ever acceptable to us; they pour balm into my heart.

Fare Thee well, my dearest Mother. Was my Samuel here, he would unite in the salutation of tender and endeared love to my Father, thyself, and dear Boy, with thy dutiful and affectionate daughter, S. Hoare.

Letter from Samuel Hoare, Jr., to John Gurney.

Norwich, August 29th, 1771.

Dear John,

As I am sensible how much a continued series of amusement and diversion relaxes our attention to the most important duty of life, that of answering the purpose for which we were created,—" to glorify God by our free obedience," I am excited by a sincere regard to thy present and future happiness, to transmit to thee this token of unfeigned affection, in full confidence of thy generosity in exercising my freedom, if it should prove unacceptable, especially when thou considerest the motive that dictates it.

The various temptations to which those of our age are subjected, render an habitual state of watchfulness highly necessary for our preservation in the paths of virtue, which are the paths of peace, and unless we are continually engaged to wait for a renewal of strength to support and succour us, we shall experience the work of the Adversary on our depraved nature, till he gains the ascendant over our affections by alluring us with the engaging vanities and fading enjoyments of this transitory world, which naturally tend to a forgetfulness of duty in those who at seasons are anxiously concerned to seek an incorruptible inheritance in glory, and desire to become travellers in the road to the New Jerusalem

May we be of the happy number of those who, in the early part of our lives, are engaged to offer up an acceptable sacrifice to Him who is ever worthy the tribute of a devoted heart ; that we may fix our affections and dependence singly upon Him and not reason with flesh and blood, but willingly and with cheerfulness forsake all things which he requires at our hands, that by mortifying the gratifications of sense, we may happily attain that state of the glorious representation of the " Woman who was clothed with the Sun, and had the Moon at her feet."

But I am sensible that the desire of pleasing, and a fear of scorn and reproach have been a stumbling-block to many, and prevented the progress of that increase in the truth, and establishment in the faith, many of us would otherwise have experienced   And altho' we know that no crown can be obtained without a cross, yet, so great is our frailty and weakness, that we have not fortitude enough to forego the present pleasure of which daily observation teaches us the emptiness tho' we are no doubt sensible of the little comparison it bears with those celestial emanations which flow from the Divine Presence, and can say with King David, " One day in Thy courts is better than a thousand, I had rather be a doorkeeper in the House of the Lord, than to dwell in the tents of wickedness "

How many assent with full purpose of heart to these solemn truths, but how few live as if they really believed them !

We who, I gratefully acknowledge, have had an education superior to the greater part of mankind, and were early initiated in virtuous sentiments, ought more particularly to submit to the will of our Benefactor with an implicit obedience ; for except our righteousness exceed those who have not had these advantages, how can we expect to be accepted of him who rewards every man according to his works, justly proportionate to the talent afforded.

I fear lest we should be looking too much outward, and measuring our actions by other men's balance, which will not avail us, but rather tend to hinder our progress in the Christian warfare, and retard the operation of that power which would redeem us from sin, and purify our hearts so that we may be enabled to worship God in the " Beauty of Holiness."

That this may be not only our happy lot and portion, but that of all created beings, is the sincere prayer of thy affec' Frd and well-wisher, SAMUEL HOARE, Junr

P S.—I hope thou hast had an agreeable passage, and art well satisfied with thy excursion, which be assured, will give me pleasure to hear from thee.　Your family are all well; they have no intelligence to communicate.　My remembrance to thy two companions, tho' personally unknown to them

To Jan Vanderwerf' J⁺ Merchants in Amsterdam.　　　　For J Gurney.

' Jan Vanderwerf, Janzoon (son of Jan Vanderwerf)

INDEX.

Ped. = Pedigree.　　Pl. = Plate.

HEADLEY BROTHERS, BISHOPSGATE, E.C, AND ASHFORD, KENT.

Lightning Source UK Ltd.
Milton Keynes UK
UKHW020738200722
406119UK00005B/606